More praise for Richard Sennett's
Respect in a World of Inequality

"The liveliness of this book reflects the vivacity of its author. . . . [Respect] is part autobiography, part urban sociology, part moral philosophy, and wholly engrossing."

—Alan Ryan, *New York Review of Books*

"This is the voice of a prophet not a wonk. . . . We have plenty of wonks already, though, offering more than enough simple answers—so perhaps Sennett can play a useful role in retailoring the questions."

—Scott McLemee, *Washington Post Book World*

"Chiefly known for his elegant and scholarly writing . . . Sennett's knowledge spans the disciplines of architecture, design, music, art, literature, history, and political and economic theory, but he adds to all that a rare anthropological hunger for the details of human experience . . . he possesses a rare genius for getting into other people's heads and hearts."

—*The Guardian* (London)

"Richard Sennett has once again shown himself the master of interpretive sociology . . . provocative, insightful, and graceful in style. His elegance and brilliance are unique, particularly in the way he frames issues and provokes us to think about them in unusual new ways."

—Leon Botstein, author of *Jefferson's Children*,
president of Bard College

"A thoughtful, often personal reflection on what is wrong with welfare and with the inequities it was intended to reduce."
—Edmund Fawcett, *Times Literary Supplement*

"This is an important book that reflects the temper of our times . . . beautifully crafted." —Frank Furedi, *New Statesman*

"Absorbing and often enlightening . . . 'respect' here stands for an eroding 'caring society,' for the basis of equal opportunity, for the recognition of individual autonomy, even or especially in those condemned to 'dependency.' . . . [Sennett] writes reflectively and often beautifully."
—Roy Foster, *Financial Times*

"Sennett's book provides a compelling . . . extensive . . . fascinating exegesis of the political and religious underpinnings of charity and welfare."
—*New York*

"Sennett has mined his life, his music, and the world of ideas to produce a set of brilliant disturbances, each one shedding light on the next until finally he and the reader come to a new appreciation of autonomy and a more useful understanding of equality . . . a soulful and scholarly book."
—Earl Shorris, author of *Riches for the Poor*

"With smooth gallant strides he bounds between his own experience, the contemporary urban scene and the philosophical origins of welfare policy. . . . Sennett operates like an architect of sympathy: master-planner for a model of mutual regard that may remove the sting of social distinction."

—Boyd Tonkin, *Independent*

"In this highly rewarding book, Sennett considers the inequalities of modern society from a distinctive angle. Instead of focusing just on financial inequalities, he looks at the inequalities that exist in what he calls 'respect.' . . . Sennett is particularly good at tracing why the poor in the West might be less respected today than they were in feudal times. Wise and humane . . . Sennett has set his sights on that most daring of missions: to make the world a better place."

—Alain de Botton, *Daily Telegraph* (London)

"[Richard Sennett's] mixture of memoir and analysis explore the notion of respect . . . a carefully reasoned, insightful look at a subject that is too little understood." —*Booklist*

"Sennett's unusual series of essays . . . succeed in provoking thought on a worthy subject." —*Publishers Weekly*

Respect

in a
World of
Inequality

Richard Sennett

W. W. Norton & Company
New York   London

"Sext" and "Musée des Beaux Arts" from *W. H. Auden: Collected Poems* by W. H.
Auden, edited by Edward Mendelson. Copyright © 1937, 1940, 1951, 1952 and
renewed 1965, 1968 by W. H. Auden. Reprinted by permission of Random House, Inc.

For information about permission to reproduce selections from this book, write to
Permissions, W. W. Norton & Company, Inc., 500 Fifth Avenue, New York, NY 10110

Manufacturing by Quebecor Fairfield
Book design by Lovedog Studio
Production manager: Julia Druskin

LIBRARY OF CONGRESS CATALOGING-IN-PUBLICATION DATA
Sennett, Richard, 1943–
  Respect in a world of inequality / by Richard Sennett.— 1st ed.
    p. cm.
Includes bibliographical references and index.
  ISBN 0-393-05126-9
  1. Public welfare. 2. Welfare recipients—Psychology. 3. Respect. I. Title.
  HV40 .S5157 2003
  305—dc21
                                                              2002013018

ISBN 0-393-32537-7 (pbk.)

W. W. Norton & Company, Inc., 500 Fifth Avenue, New York, N.Y. 10110
www.wwnorton.com

W. W. Norton & Company Ltd., Castle House, 75/76 Wells Street, London W1T 3QT

1 2 3 4 5 6 7 8 9 0

For Victoria and Kevin,
and for Niall

. . . the growing good of the world is partly dependent on unhistoric acts; and that things are not so ill with you and me as they might have been, is half owing to the number who lived faithfully a hidden life, and rest in unvisited tombs.

— George Eliot
Middlemarch

Contents

Acknowledgments

I would like to thank Jean Starobinski for the example set by his writing, particularly *Largesse* (trans. Jane Todd, University of Chicago Press, 1997). I'm grateful to suggestions from Victoria Glendinning on the uses of autobiography; and to discussions with Eric Klinenberg, Steven Lukes, Craig Calhoun, and Saskia Sassen about sociology. Niall Hobhouse argued with me from start to finish. Murray Perahia has corrected my memory. Alexander Nahamas at Princeton and Alan Ryan at Oxford arranged occasions to present parts of this book; I thank colleagues at both places for comments. Michael Laskawy and Chryssa Kanellak-Reimer helped me do research. Stuart Proffitt at Penguin and Alane Mason at Norton have proved patient and supportive editors.

Preface

Several years ago I wrote a book about work, *The Corrosion of Character: The Personal Consequences of Work in the New Capitalism*, and I'd meant this book to be a companion volume about welfare. Welfare clients often complain of being treated without respect. But the lack of respect they experience occurs not simply because they are poor, old, or sick. Modern society lacks positive expressions of respect and recognition for others.

To be sure, society has a master idea: it is that by treating one another as equals we affirm mutual respect. However, can we only respect people who are equal in strength to ourselves? Some inequalities are arbitrary but others are intractable—such as differences of talent. People in modern society generally fail to convey mutual regard and recognition across these boundaries.

The hard counsel of equality comes home to people within the welfare system when they feel their own claims to the attention of others lie solely in their problems, in the facts of their neediness. To earn respect, they must not be weak; they must not be needy.

When welfare clients are urged to "earn" self-respect, this usually means becoming materially self-sufficient. But in the larger society self-respect depends not only on economic standing, but on what one does, how one achieves it. Self-respect cannot be "earned" in quite the same way people earn money. And again inequality intrudes; someone at the bottom of the social order can achieve self-respect but its possession is fragile.

The relation between respect and inequality has become my theme. As I began writing out my thoughts, I realized how much it has shaped my own life. I grew up in the welfare system, then escaped from it by virtue of my talents. I hadn't lost respect for those I'd left behind, but my own sense of self-worth lay in the way I'd left them behind. So I was hardly a neutral observer; were I to write an honest book on this subject I would have to write in part from my own experience. Much as I like reading memoirs by others, however, I dislike personal confession.

So this book became an experiment. It's neither a book of practical policies for the welfare state nor a full-blown autobiography. I've tried to use my own experience, rather, as a starting point for exploring a larger social problem.

Part One

Scarcity of Respect

Lack of respect, though less aggressive than an outright insult, can take an equally wounding form. No insult is offered another person, but neither is recognition extended; he or she is not *seen*—as a full human being whose presence matters.

When a society treats the mass of people in this way, singling out only a few for recognition, it creates a scarcity of respect, as though there were not enough of this precious substance to go around. Like many famines, this scarcity is man-made; unlike food, respect costs nothing. Why, then, should it be in short supply?

Chapter One

Memories of Cabrini

The Housing Project

Early in the last century, poor American blacks began to escape the serfdom of the rural South by moving to cities up North. When the Second World War began, this tide of migrants swelled; both black women and black men found industrial work in the war factories, which gave the women an alternative to domestic service. In Chicago, my native city, whites were no better disposed to blacks than down South; the appearance of these new industrial laborers prompted immigrant Poles, Greeks, and Italians to move away from the blacks, even if they all had to work together. However, the city's planners sought to break white flight from neighborhoods in which blacks settled by building new housing in the middle of Chicago, reserving a certain number of places for the white poor. Cabrini Green was such a racially mixed enclave, and it was here that I spent part of my childhood.

In later years Cabrini became an emblem for all that was worst in public housing—full of drugs and guns, its lawns carpeted in broken glass and dog shit. But in the late 1940s, the architecture of this housing project would have seemed to an outsider simply dull—plain long, low boxes without any softening ornament. The plumbing worked, the lawns were green, there were good schools nearby. Indeed, for blacks coming to Chicago, "the future seemed bright," one observer later said of a project like ours; these cinder-block houses replaced the tar-paper shacks in which many people had lived in the South, the projects sending a signal that the larger society at last recognized their historic plight.[1] "Back then," my neighbor Gloria Hayes Morgan has written, "the Frances Cabrini Homes were just clean cheap housing that families were glad to have until they could do better."[2]

To the poor in Cabrini Green who were white, however, public housing sent a different signal.

Racial strife had a long history in Chicago; by the Second World War the authorities knew they had to address it. When Cabrini opened in 1942, the authorities proposed to the poor white: if you will live in the midst of blacks, we will take care of your rent. The war had created a housing shortage in the city, particularly of cheap housing. Like government planners before and since, the designers of Cabrini Green sought to remedy a large social evil in meeting that practical welfare need, using housing as a "tool" for combating racial segregation. It was not a tool they wielded directly; to my knowledge, none of the creators of Cabrini Green actually lived among us. Nor did the city's then small black bourgeoisie live here. I do not know if our neighbors were more or less racist than other whites. But whatever their views, they had become the servants of racial inclusion as imagined by a superior class.

Originally Cabrini was meant to be 75 percent white and 25 percent black. By the time it opened its doors, those percentages were reversed.[3] My mother remembered many middle-class white people driven by the housing shortage into the project, but statistically, middle-class residents were few in number and the first to escape.[4] Other whites, destined to stay longer in Cabrini Green, included wounded war veterans who could not work full-time, and the authorities had also lodged among us some mental patients not ill enough to remain in hospital but too fragile to live on their own. This mixed community of blacks, the white poor, the wounded, and the deranged framed the subjects of the experiment in social inclusion.

There was nothing peculiarly American in the effort to use housing for the poor as a laboratory for unresolved problems in the larger society. In Britain, Jeremy Bentham had, early in the nineteenth century, imagined that new workers' housing might serve as an exemplar of a more cohesive, integrated society; the British Artisans' and Labourers' Dwelling Act of 1868 aimed to show how market capitalism might be tamed through shaping the physical fabric of the city. The first Peabody Trust housing conducted architectural experiments in how "to design a life, not just a house." All these British efforts focused on class. Cabrini and similar American housing developments in the twentieth century were special in that they sought to treat together two equally large, gaping social wounds: race and class.[5]

I should perhaps explain why my mother, who came from yet another kind of background, came to live in the project. The daughter of a brilliant but eccentric inventor—my grandfather worked out the mechanism of the phone-answering machine but never bothered to patent it—my mother spent her youth in the turbulence of radical politics and artistic experiment of the Great Depression. She was politically committed, but she wanted to write, and what she wanted to write was good sentences whether political or not.

In the mid-1930s she met my father, who shortly thereafter departed for the Spanish Civil War with his brother, the most politically inflamed member of our family. The war against fascism in Spain drew idealistic soldiers from around the world; many went home disillusioned by communism, a disillusion capped by the Hitler-Stalin Pact of 1939. So it was for my father, whose personal life became unstrung. In an effort to hold their marriage together, my parents conceived me, and as so often happens in such cases, my birth proved the end of their marriage. My father fled when I was a few months old—I never met him—and my mother was financially down on her luck. Since her youth she had written plays and short stories; now there was no money for that. We moved to Cabrini in 1946, when I was three.

With one exception, I've necessarily had to reconstruct the years we spent there from the memoirs of others, from official documents, and particularly from my mother's writings.

In a memoir my mother wrote about Cabrini, for instance, she recalled our own apartment: "two rooms and a bath . . . at the entrance to the bedroom stood a coal stove, and several times a day I shook the ashes through and swept the living room floor. . . ."[6] What initially struck her, though, was the noise outside. The apartment seemed "like a beleaguered ship. Around it, from early morning until far into evening, there rose a sea of sound . . . voices screaming, laughing, wailing, shouting."[7] The taxi driver who initially transported us to Cabrini could not believe, my mother said, that a nice young woman and child would be moving there.

My mother remembered me, after eighteen months there, as a boy who was "unusually large, and seems older than five, with a thoughtful, serious face."[8] In two years, my size would be the saving of me in the streets. My seriousness would also prove the saving of me; I loved listening to music and learning to read. My mother had begun the career which would eventually make her a distinguished social worker. We may well have seemed strange to our new neighbors, the two rooms filled with books and classical music. I imagine, moreover, that our temporary poverty did not carry the same stigma it might have inflicted on many of our white neighbors.

That stigma could be measured by the geography of the city. Cabrini Green was only eight city blocks west of Chicago's "Gold Coast"; this was and remains a ribbon of high-rise apartments for the wealthy which runs along Lake Michigan. The Gold Coast was simply too rich to count in most people's reckonings of their social standing.[9] To the west of the project, however, space meant more. Just beyond Cabrini Green lay the mosaic of neighborhoods in which the European immigrants to Chicago had first settled, streets on which people still spoke German, Polish, or Greek. Farther west were the beginnings of suburban developments to which the children of the immigrants began migrating after the Second World War: here could be found houses with garages, with bits of private lawn— signs a family was rising into the lower middle class.

The whites in our housing project had little prospect of moving west. Many, as I say, were people who had not managed to pull themselves together from the stresses of the Great Depression in the 1930s or from the war. Their cousins visited the project on weekends, parking the enormous American automobiles of the time in front of our concrete boxes, cars we children surrounded and stroked like pets.

Everyone in Cabrini had a passive relationship to the project because of its architecture. None of the residents had a hand in designing where we lived. The plan itself was a rigid grid of low-rise houses; the lawns and open spaces outside admitted no gardening by the residents. Next to Cabrini there was added fifteen years later a group of high-rise buildings, called the Robert Taylor Homes. These new building were designed to be even more directive, their elevators guarded, their floor layout dictating where beds, tables, and sofas could be placed.

Given the horror the project later became, I want to emphasize the positive side of these controls; as in Viennese workers' housing from the 1920s, these Chicago architectural severities symbolized something new and clean, a designer's modernist flag.

Passivity of a more social sort, however, was also imposed, and this was more likely to dent people's self-respect. The inhabitants of Cabrini Green and the Robert Taylor Homes were not allowed to choose their neighbors; that decision was made for them by the Chicago Housing Authority, a judgment made of the tenant's character as well as of his or her cash. Evidently there was a tenants' committee, but it was permitted few powers; my aunt later told me that the officials who mattered in running the project seldom bothered to attend its meetings.

I have one sharp memory of my own from these years, an incident of racial violence in the project between black and white children a little older than I was, occurring just before we first left the project, when I was seven.

Several of the buildings ringing Cabrini Green had been abandoned, their empty rooms full of broken windows and building waste. Here, in facing empty tenements, white children hid in rooms on one side of the street, black children on the other, in order to play the game of "glass wars." The game involved slinging panes of glass across the street, like skipping stones across the water; when you cut someone on the other side, you scored a point.

For children the glass wars more provided the pleasure of physical violence than expressed racial hate; Gloria Morgan writes that within the project there was "just enough static in the air to generate occasional friction" in the racial climate.[10] The thrill of the glass wars was the blood. Players scored few points directly, since it was easy to peer outside and see the glass coming. The game became dangerous when errant panes shattered against the back walls of the rooms; players got shards of glass stuck in their ankles or hands.

Once, however, a young black girl nearly died of a cut to her neck. Her teammates got her to a hospital by flagging down a passing bus; the hospital called not the parents but the police, the police again called the school rather than the parents, the school called out a platoon of social workers, who descended upon the community. The parents thus learned about the incident only after it was over, managed by professionals.

My aunt later cited this incident to me as one reason why my mother became desperate to move out. Evidently our white neighbors were angry at the authorities for interfering; the black parents were more angry at their own children for attracting the attention of the authorities. The difference makes sense. Down South, an incident like this could have sparked off attacks on black adults; the demons of racism could be roused no matter who was the victim. For the Chicago whites, the problem was that the authorities had usurped the parental role; other adults had stepped in first.

When I returned to Chicago for university, an elderly teacher in the local school told me that she remembered the incident quite well, because the white parents had turned on her, believing she had known about the fights all along but kept it from them. Years later, when interviewing white working-class families in Boston, I noticed a peculiar turn of phrase to express this conviction. It was use of the word "them" as equally applicable to poor blacks and to liberal, middle-class professionals like teachers and social workers. The usage confounds race and class, marking "them" as a single invasive threat; it expresses a working-class fear of vulnerability. In Boston, white workers fought "them" in resisting for decades forced racial integration in schools. In Chicago, the whites in Cabrini Green had accepted cheap, integrated housing; no high wall could protect "us" from "them."

Fifty years later, with all the distortions and whatever wisdom of hindsight, it appears to me that Cabrini posed two problems which could challenge its residents' sense of self-worth. One was adult dependence, a condition which American adults tend to fear as demeaning; "welfare dependency" is a synonym for humiliation. Race shaped that humiliating dependence in Cabrini; the need of our white neighbors for housing forced them into racial relations which more privileged whites avoided.

The other problem was that the project denied people control over their own lives. They were rendered spectators to their own needs, mere consumers of care provided to them. It was here that they experienced that peculiar lack of respect which consists of not being seen, not being accounted as full human beings. The aftermath of the glass wars signaled that invisibility to the whites in the project; to blacks, such scarcity of respect was an age-old condition.

Escape

With an American turn of the social kaleidoscope, our fortunes slowly improved. When we left Cabrini, my still-single mother began to make her way as a social worker and my music began to flourish. Though no boy prodigy, I composed, played the cello, and started performing. It was through learning an art that I began to leave others behind.

Time speeds up in the experience of serious child musicians; by the age or eleven or twelve, you have to spend four or five hours a day practicing; if at the onset of adolescence you also begin performing, the work of adult life has already begun. The hours I spent practicing were hours not spent playing with other children; at fifteen, when I began playing in public, my colleague friends were older musicians, in university or beyond. Thanks to this forcing of time, I thought I'd become a new person, and Cabrini no longer seemed connected to me.

Ambition is usually taken to be the driving force of self-made men and women, and I certainly had my full share of it. But the development of any talent involves an element of craft, of doing something well for its own sake, and it is this craft element which provides the individual with an inner sense of self-respect. It's not so much a matter of getting ahead as of becoming inside. The craft of music made that gift to me.

Perhaps I can make this concrete by describing an act of bodily mastery every cellist must acquire. Vibrato is a rocking motion of the left hand on a string which colors a note around its precise pitch; waves of sound spread out in vibrato like ripples from a pool into which one has thrown a stone. Vibrato begins at the elbow, the impulse to rock starting from that anchor, passing through the forearm into the palm of the hand and then through the finger.

The craft element is this: vibrato requires that a cellist first master the capacity to play perfectly in tune. If a young cellist lacks that mastery, every time he or she vibrates, the note will sound sour, accentuating the inaccuracy of pitch and skewing the note's overtones; precise pitch is our version of artistic truth. Freedom to vibrate depends on that discipline, whereas purely impulsive expression produces just mess—a piece of folk wisdom which applies to both hand and heart.

I was blessed with a good ear and quickly played in tune, but even so it took me several years to achieve an easy vibrato. At twelve, when this finally occurred, it was an epochal event for me, as important as being good at games would be for another child. And as in sports, this event has two sides: the respect one earns from others for doing something well, and the act of exploring how to do something. There's satisfaction in that—by constructing an accurate, free sound I experienced a profound pleasure in and for itself, and a sense of self-worth which didn't depend on others.

After a decade, the need of more musical training brought

me back to Chicago in 1960, aged seventeen. Frank Miller, a cellist in the Chicago Symphony, took me on as a private student, and I enrolled in the university; though music was to be my career, I also wanted some general education. For a year and a half in Chicago, Frank Miller gently, relentlessly drove me; I worked up a program of modern but accessible music— the Barber cello sonata, salon music of Poulenc—which Miller forced me to treat as seriously as Bach or Beethoven.

He then sent me to New York to study conducting with a colleague. Miller, himself a great cellist, cherished the desire to follow as a conductor in the footsteps of his master, Toscanini; for reasons I don't fully understand, there is a close connection between our instrument and conducting.

I spent nine months in Greenwich Village, living with another boy and girl in a one-room flat near a transvestite bar while preparing to conduct a performance of Bizet's *Carmen*. Like many musicians, I was a late-night person, and this bit of New York was open twenty-four hours a day; at dawn the bar offered food, cigarettes, and spectacle. But this was simply relief. I was hard at work then trying to master the "Monteux box," a conducting technique pioneered by Pierre Monteux which contains the conductor's hands within a small imaginary box at shoulder level, so that every gesture counts no matter how small. My most vivid visual memory of New York at this time was of my bathroom and its mirror, before which I practiced the Monteux box.

It was in New York that I also learned the limits of my musical gift. When I listened to friends like the pianists Murray Perahia or Richard Goode play, I heard something beyond my own grasp of music; they shaped air-pauses and other aspects of phrasing, as well as brought out unexpected harmonic voices, which I never would. The craft labor of music teaches objective measures of what one hears, and in time I accepted that I lacked their art.

Were it true that we only do things well in order to compete with or earn the regard of others, then such an experience of limits should lessen our involvement in what we do. But this calculating view is superficial. Though it tempered my conceit, learning my limits didn't erode my love of music—and I think this is true of most other people who develop a genuine craft-love. But there is a real divide here in the meaning of "respect" itself, between the social and the personal, between being respected and feeling what one does is inherently worthwhile.

I left New York, chastened but not discouraged, because the Vietnam War cast its shadow over me in 1963, as it did over many other young men; I would be drafted to fight in the war if I did not return full-time to a proper university. I returned to dutiful labor in Miller's studio, and enrolled at the university in a course of historical studies, a subject I wrongly assumed would leave me plenty of time for music. At this point, Chicago began to shake my inwardness.

My Mother's Reserve

My mother and I had returned together to Cabrini just once, in 1959. No white people were then anywhere visible. But it was the physical ruin of the place which struck us; gone was the obsessive neatness of both black and white apartments a decade before. The musician Ramsey Lewis, a contemporary of mine in Cabrini, remembers that once "we were quite proud of the flowers in the front and the vegetable gardens and grass in the back."[11] Now that pride had disappeared.

In a short story about our return, my mother wrote that she was particularly shocked by the ruined playground, now "buried in a jungle of fifteen-storied behemoths which stretched for miles"—the high-rise project called Robert Taylor Homes had opened its doors in 1956—and even more by our own house: "When we found the cinder-covered playground enclosed with cyclone fencing, we found our former home. . . . Our door was a dingier red. Frayed curtains hung in its grimy windows. We could not see anyone within."[12]

However, the upset she records in her story was not evident at the time; my mother looked around as though she were studying the facts. My own reactions, as I remember them, do not do me much credit; I hated what I saw, harbored no sympathy for people whose lives appeared so visibly to have fallen apart. But my mother's response, as I would learn, was not cold like mine. She was, in her reserve, in her avoidance of sentimentality, expressing a kind of respect for those forced to inhabit this spectacle of poverty.

"Learning race is like learning a language," remarks the sociologist Dalton Conley. His upbringing was much like mine, and he means the white race-speaker eventually becomes "stripped of any illusions . . . of being like other kids."[13] In Chicago in the 1960s, that was true for both black and white adults. Chicago, like all northern American cities, had long been segregated in fact if not in law. The space of the city was divided by race; so was its lived time. During the day, the races might mingle, particularly in the department stores in the Loop, the center of the city; at night, the races almost never met.

Among the poor blacks of Ramsey Lewis's generation who moved up socially there had been at least the hope that the worst effects of racial segregation could be overcome, such as access to the medical care available to whites, or to white universities. The civil rights movement attempted to cross that divide of inequality in northern cities, but at the same time middle-class blacks were also being "stripped of any illusions" that upward economic mobility alone would suffice for social acceptance.

When I returned from New York to Chicago in 1963, I found one small corner where racial differences were bridged in some of the places where I performed. It's a stereotype to imagine black churches only filled with gospel singing; the more middle-class churches of my youth often programmed music like the Bach cantatas hard to schedule in a concert hall. There were a few young, black classical musicians in the city as well, and we tended to meet at these church events. While the audiences in both jazz clubs and concert halls in Chicago were beginning to go gray, in the small religious venues where young musicians were likely to play, the ages as well as the races mixed among a usually tiny public.

In 1964, at a church near Cabrini one wintry morning, I played in a concert to which a teacher from my old school came. The glass wars were only a minor foretaste of the racial violence which spread throughout the West Side of Chicago in the late 1940s and 1950s, yet she had hung on to the community. My old teacher's companion at the concert was a young black woman perhaps ten years older than me, a professional welfare worker, well-spoken and well-dressed. She obviously didn't belong to the community she served. Perhaps because of this, she jolted me into seeing for the first time my mother as a working adult, independent of me.

Like all children, I'd taken my mother's work for granted. But why had she chosen social work in particular? In a short story my mother wrote about a young social worker, her leading character "had the feeling that somewhere, quite close, but just out of reach, significant things were happening."[14] As a professional, my mother kept that feeling of involvement locked up; hers was no passionate embrace of the oppressed, she was precise and calm in her work, firmly marking out human distances.

This short story revealed equally an inner unease and anxiety about her work invisible to me as a child: the protagonist dreads one night making a home visit to a welfare mother the next day, hating her role as "the investigator."[15] As a child, I could not sense any of this because my mother's voice and gestures took on a different character whenever she was called by business to the phone, or entertained colleagues at home—the same character as on her return visit to Cabrini.

Sometimes in our experience, the curtains momentarily part to reveal a scene we know contains an important clue—about something—but then as rapidly they close before we can make out what has been disclosed. The young black social worker, my mother's professional daughter, drew back the curtain on a scene illustrating compassion. I wasn't so much struck by the fact that both were giving of themselves to others. In my unregenerate male state, I assumed this was just what women did. It was rather how little "motherly" either woman was, the fact of their reserve. When I asked the young social worker about Cabrini, she spoke the language I'd heard my mother use to colleagues, filled with phrases like "deprivation syndromes" and "low-esteem anxieties."

This social-work jargon can certainly be demeaning, treating the poor like damaged goods, or can descend into ludicrous psychobabble. But for a moment I saw it was something else as well.

Both my mother and her professional daughter were people of a higher class who had the power to violate the poor, as my mother wrote; if they had dedicated their lives to the poor, charity itself has the power to wound; pity can beget contempt; compassion can be intimately linked to inequality. To make compassion work, perhaps it was necessary to defuse sentiment, to deal coolly with others. Crossing the boundary of inequality might require reserve on the part of the stronger person making the passage; reserve would acknowledge the difficulty, distance could make a signal of respect, if a peculiar one.

All I could understand at the concert was that the young social worker's cool words had a reason, a justifying necessity. Perhaps this momentary disclosure stuck in my mind because of a change in my own life.

When I returned to Chicago, aged twenty, I had my first real love affair; though precocious in music, I was not in sex. My companion was a black student of philosophy. Playful and funny about friends, she was dead serious about Immanuel Kant. Night for us had a different structure in Chicago than it had for me alone in New York; after studying, practicing, making love, we set forth in search of food, but almost no restaurant would have us. The white restaurants explicitly refused a mixed couple, while at the black restaurants we simply waited and waited for empty tables mysteriously "reserved" to become free. We usually gravitated to an unsegregated restaurant, the Tropical Hut; over rice laced with a sugary sauce my friend emphasized the key Immanuel Kant held to all philosophy, I railed against the neglect of the music of Gabriel Fauré.

Though neither of us was political, we used occasionally to drop into the office of a civil rights organization where we had friends. The young whites in civil rights organizations of the early 1960s were an idealistic breed; they gave their time and sometimes risked their lives. But in the civil rights office the atmosphere crackled with internal tension. "Learning race" was coupled to the questions "Why are you helping me? Why are you personally so committed?" Any answer that betrayed pity for poor blacks could be taken as condescension. The whites were caught between commitment and the fear of giving offense.

Though I didn't realize it then, our visits to the civil rights office raised the curtain on the same dilemma my mother and the young social worker faced: how to cross the boundaries of inequality with mutual respect. One could say that these civil rights workers behaved in a contrary spirit to the social workers who invaded the privacy of white families after the glass wars; like my mother's sort of social worker, the young whites held themselves back. But in both cases, true mutuality was lacking, the mutuality of the freely spoken. Silence, caution, and the fear of offending ruled instead.

Thanks to my own affair, I began at least to feel the undercurrents of humiliation to which my partner was exposed. After a few months of Kant and Fauré, she came under pressure from political blacks to give me up, pressure put on her even by black men with trophy blondes in tow; our relation was said to mirror the slave master and his servant woman.

At first we stopped appearing in public together. But in a few months we returned to the Tropical Hut, though never to the civil rights office. Her pride affronted, she held herself aloof from the mounting struggle. In an era when the label "young black woman philosopher" referred to very few people, she undoubtedly felt both isolated and confused. I answered her increasingly bad temper with my own, and by the time I left university our affair had ended.

When I try to thread these events together now, the reserve and silences my mother practiced seem to me to extend beyond the domain of social work. It takes a long time, and a great deal of trust, for highly educated professionals and unskilled laborers to speak freely to one another; the beautiful and the ugly don't talk easily to each other about their bodies; people whose lives are full of adventure have trouble "relating" to the experience of people constrained within narrow routines.

Inequality can breed unease, unease breed a desire to connect, yet the connection itself be of a tacit, silent, reserved sort. This emotional chain of events complicates the precept to "show respect" for someone else lower down the social or economic ladder. People may feel that esteem yet fear to seem condescending, and so hold back. Moreover, awareness of one's own privileges can arouse unease; in modern society people do not speak easily of their superior station in life, as they did in the *ancien régime* unabashedly of their superior station. Paradoxically, the anxiety of privilege may sharpen awareness of those who have less—an anxiety one would not easily declare.

For these reasons, feeling respect may not lead to showing

respect. I don't say my mother failed in this; rather, she was caught in a dilemma not of her own making.

My Left Hand

So far I've touched on three themes: the demeaning effects of adult dependence, the difference between self-respect and recognition from others, the difficulty of showing mutual respect across the boundaries of inequality. The themes are broad, my experience of them particular but not unique. The next part of my own story is singular; it has to do with how I lost the craft upon which I'd built my self-respect. I record this event because it taught me something which has perhaps a larger resonance: how loss of confidence in oneself can make one more aware of others.

Early in 1962 I began to have trouble closing my left hand; increasingly I had to strain to push down the strings of the cello, and the physical strain began to sound in the music I played. This was particularly true of my vibrato; from being liquid and free, it became increasingly tense, as the link between my elbow and fingertips was broken. Up to this year I had seldom experienced stage fright. Now, as my left hand stiffened, I began to suffer from nerves before concerts, my stomach also tightening up. When I went to New York to prepare for conducting lessons, I thought I would give the left hand a break, but the rest didn't seem to help.

It's long been the fashion to consider artists prone to neurosis, even though the practical demands of a working musician's life require good self-discipline and calm under pressure, sanity enough. I succumbed to the fashion in accepting for a while that my psyche was staging some sort of protest through my hand. In 1964, the pianist Rudolph Serkin set me straight.

He'd seen the problem many times before: the tendons of my left hand were tightening like the strings of a cello being tuned up too high; in order to solve the problem I needed to loosen the tendons' pegs; for that I would need an operation, and he gave me the name of a doctor. The concert I gave in the church near Cabrini was one of my last before this operation in 1964. Unfortunately, it went wrong; until the advent of microsurgery such operations tended to be chancy affairs. The result was that my left hand now could close only slowly; it worked well enough for ordinary tasks, but my career as a cellist had for all practical purposes, at age twenty-one, ended.

I was not immediately prepared to face up to my predicament; indeed, at first I handled it badly. I blamed the surgeon. Worse, I withdrew from my mother. She had left me free enough as a child, but did worry aloud and frequently about how I'd make a living from music, speculating on what I'd eventually do instead; no evidence sufficed to allay her doubt. Now the bandaged hand seemed to prove her right, and I stopped speaking frankly with her, minimizing the gravity of the event and obscuring its outcome. My companion had also to bear bouts of operatic self-pity, part of the price she had paid for staying with me.

Of course, the sun still rose every morning and people continued dusting their windowsills. A few months after the event I started to put myself right and consider what to do. Conducting might have served as a ready replacement, and I had the ready example in my college friend Leon Botstein, today both a distinguished conductor and a university president, then a violinist just beginning to move from the orchestra chair to the podium.

But the operation triggered in me the recognition that I did not want to take up this alternative. To conduct seriously seemed to imply starting all over again; as the bandages came off and I began exercise therapy, I realized I lacked the will. Like many people who have spent childhood as musicians rather than as children, I had perhaps been used up by the obsessional energy it required.

Since I had returned to Chicago, the world outside my own orbit also had begun to tug at me. People in my social milieu were all engaged in causes—my mother, her younger sister and brother-in-law, and family friends involved themselves as social workers, labor arbitrators, teachers in schools for the poor. The racial conflicts I'd experienced in my love affair had disconcerted me; no beautiful notes would assuage them. Most of all, the Vietnam War made decision urgent. My draft board would not allow my impaired hand as a medical exemption; it worked well enough to fire a gun.

Avoiding the Vietnam War was the pivotal fact of life for young men of my generation, an avoidance which was in one way truly shameful. When people like me didn't fight, others who were poorer were forced to take our places. The ready answer we had was that the war shouldn't be fought at all— which was true enough, but still, making someone else do the fighting was an elite privilege. For young people of my generation, the reckoning of what our privilege cost others came only when the soldiers returned from Vietnam, dazed and frequently drug-addicted.

I was able to escape the war thanks to the sociologist David

Riesman. His elder daughter was a singer, and through her I came to know him. We had always got on well; he liked talking to young people, and I was full of talk; hearing of my difficulties, he took me on as a research student at Harvard.

This was not so surprising as it may now seem. Harvard was then fairly relaxed about admitting students, open to taking on a few young people who were, we then put it, in the throes of an "identity crisis." Cambridge, Massachusetts, itself preserved forty years ago the look of a comfortable New England small town, filled with wooden houses, simple in design even when they were big. The dust-free light, especially in the fall, played off the wooden surfaces, clarifying their planes. I entered the academy believing it could be similarly clarifying.

Even while studying music with Frank Miller I was, as I've said, formally enrolled in a history program at the University of Chicago. I now decided to continue this work, focusing on the history of cities. The subject interested me then, and has ever since, but I decided too quickly. Having lost one discipline, I simply shoved another in its place—not facing up to the fact I did not really know what I wanted to do.

My hand injury proved a danger to me at Harvard, just because it was so seductive a story to others. During seminars I'd replay in my mind old pieces, rebowing or refingering them; friends noted my fingers move involuntarily during these discussions; the artist deprived of his art was an appealing figure to them. Only in my third year, when I left off recounting my sad story, did I really begin addressing the consequences of my hand injury, which were that I didn't know what to do with myself.

Knowing what to do with oneself can, of course, become a trap. The craft competence children develop is strongly related to play, like learning how to master a game; there's little need to measure its ultimate purpose or value. Purely functional competence of this sort can later damage the life of a young adult. Society in the person of parents and teachers may approve the functional choice, but the young adult knows it is too easy; complex desires, the noise of life, may be shut out. The adolescent who knows exactly what he or she wants may often be a limited human being. But my own self-doubts were contained within the shell of the "counterculture" of the 1960s.

The counterculture mounted an attack on discipline in theory and in practice. The political philosopher Marshall Berman, as a young man, reveled in "the sense of being caught up in a vortex where all facts and values are whirled, exploded, decomposed, recombined; a basic uncertainty about what is basic, what is valuable, what is real."[16] Students for a Democratic Society, an organization which spoke for our generation, has been described by the historian James Miller as given over to "spontaneity, imagination, passion, playfulness, movement— the sensation of being on edge, at the limits of freedom."[17]

The counterculture's attack on security of self also had an accusatory streak: why can't you let go? That accusation particularly cut young musicians; our training had been both narrow and relentless. Moreover, our particular art seemed to have no place in our own times. In the 1960s, America was still filled with exiles who clung to the European past; classical music was an important part of that memory, an art which came from another time and another place. This musical culture clashed with the counterculture of youth.

I remember being immersed with the conductor Carl Schachter the middle of the 1960s—seated in one of the delis on

New York's Upper West Side which then catered to musicians by serving, rudely, immense amounts of cheap kosher food—in one of those conversations about Art and Life which only young people can conduct without irony. Specifically, what "relevance" did Schubert have to imperialism? In the end Carl gave up on this question and returned to practice in his studio. But for him and, I think, most classical musicians of my generation, the ill fit between culture and counterculture, the uncertainty about inheriting an art, was positive. Questioning the role of their art broadened musicians as human beings.

But we still had the anchor of a demanding art. Looking back, I understand a little better one philosophical source of the desire to be free of that discipline. The Renaissance philosopher Pico della Mirandola, in his *Oration on the Dignity of Man*, formulated the dictum of "Man as his own Maker," which meant self-formation as an exploration rather than following a recipe. Religion, family, community, Pico argued, set the scene, but one has to write the script for oneself.

In some dim way, my generation affirmed this view, but ignored in their own lives the warning Pico had issued: one needs to create a cohering life story. "Dropping out" might be a badge of honor, but solved nothing about making a life. Wandering free at twenty, by age thirty many in my generation frequently felt they'd missed something; the life narrative did not move forward.

Though I swam happily in the sexual currents of the 1960s, I was fundamentally an unliberated soul; at school I wanted security, not adventure. I was partly prevented from burying myself in the library, however, by Riesman and his colleague Erik Erikson.

Erikson had in his own past taken a turn somewhat like my own; he'd begun as an artist making woodcut prints, which he then abandoned for psychoanalysis. He remained intensely visual, often staring at other people to understand them without being aware of how discomfiting his gaze could be. He had no medical training, and in the 1960s psychoanalysis was becoming a doctor's specialty. Erikson thought this medical turn diminished the cultural scope of analysis; he was hard on young doctors, and looked more favorably on students who fainted at the sight of blood. So he had at Harvard many students like me who were less professionally, more personally searching. What most struck me about him was a quality all good clinicians possess, his capacity to listen steadily as we thrashed about, Erikson puffing on the small Danish cigars he then favored but remaining otherwise immobile.

Riesman, on the contrary, was filled with evident anxiety. A letter of a few lines to him would bring back pages in response, as if he worried that he might fail you by leaving any possible nuance unaddressed. Thanks to his book *The Lonely Crowd*, Riesman was famous, and his nerves may have in part come from this; he didn't quite believe his reviews. Like Erikson he taught what he was not trained for, Riesman having begun as a lawyer. But still his self-doubt was sad; he had written a truly great book. His nervousness struck me all the more in that his daughter, as a singer, was all ease; her shoulders down, an unforced sound poured out of her.

More vulnerable than Erikson, Riesman was to me more sympathetic. But at Harvard his responsive anxiety did him harm. In those days Great Men (and they were mostly men) deigned to impart their wisdom in lectures but otherwise had scant contact with their students. Riesman behaved much better. He believed in face-to-face contact even though hundreds of young people filled his lecture hall; he spent hours in his office dictating letters to these students about their papers—occupying the time of two harried secretaries—and his door was never closed. Responsiveness was his obsession, and it used him up.

Erikson and Riesman were friends, or perhaps it's better said that they were complicit; for different reasons both felt outsiders in that bastion of official thought. As teachers, neither was disposed to point the way forward along a clear path. Erikson pondered to himself when he lectured; Riesman suggested twenty books you might read, and ten people whom you should telephone, to pursue whatever it was you were pursuing.

Each in his own way, Erikson and Riesman felt oppressed by the waste of life which surrounded them in Harvard, a university filled with so many very bright kids. Erikson remarked one evening, "You pass through an identity crisis, you don't dwell in it." Many of Riesman's most political students had turned on him, rather than accepting who he was and going their own way. Uniquely lacking in reserve, compulsively open, he became their prey: he was a "liberal" in the hated sense of seeing all sides, engaging all sides, rather than refusing and rejecting.

For the first few years I spent at Harvard, I felt only the measure of the material distance I had traveled. In the world I'd grown up in, it was hard enough to put bread on the table; because of my past, I felt comfort in Harvard's security, and I came even to enjoy its professorial pomposity, which was also reassuring.

But in time I began to understand that the experience of privilege can take more subtle forms; I began to sense, for instance, how class-bound could be the attitudes of those who attacked teachers like Riesman. Here was a world of so many helping hands, an army of tutors, counselors, and support staff stamped in Riesman's mold—the privileged young were thrown a safety net which they both scorned and took for granted. The sense of "spontaneity, imagination, passion, playfulness, movement; the sensation of being on edge, at the limits of freedom"—to recall James Miller's words about the radical youth of my generation—allowed them to assume that nothing, in the end, would really go wrong.

Later I would learn that sociologists gave names to this privileged assumption. It reflects the possession of "cultural capital," that is, of a network of connections and contacts which kept members of the network afloat; it embodies what the sociologist Robert Merton calls "the Peter principle": the higher one rises in society the less likely statistically one is to fall back. When I began to study labor, I saw this peculiar confidence in both old-boy and new-boy networks at the top of businesses, whereas the networks of people lower down were too weak to give much support.

Cast in these terms, the inequality is obvious. It was obscured in my youth because inequality was refracted through a language of personal daring and political challenge. Personal "liberation" became my generation's word for a self-confidence which did not recognize, or know, what a weight of privilege supported it. It was among young adults the opposite but equal in weight to self-confidence gained through the rigid pursuit of a career; each in its own way could produce a limited human being. Neither was viable as a long-term project for forming self-worth.

Perhaps I can broaden what I am trying to say about self-confidence and inequality by skipping ahead a few years, in describing one meeting point between my old life and my new life.

The Ones Left Behind

The city of my childhood came to be ever more on my mind at Harvard; indeed, I wrote my first book about it.[18] I had also begun to make brief trips back. A few of these were to attend mentoring sessions arranged by community groups or local churches. The events offered up "role models" to the young; successful people were meant to explain how they succeeded.[19]

The earliest meeting I attended, in 1971, has most stayed in my mind.[20] We role models sat in a row on a rostrum in a community center; about fifty kids sat ranged in chairs before us under pitiless fluorescent lighting. I was the lone white on the platform. The role model is meant just to tell his or her own story, not as a confession but as a clarifying life narrative; poor youngsters lack much understanding of how the society beyond ghetto walls works. To venture outside and survive requires more than learning how to act white or middle-class: from inside the young person has to be able to answer the question "What do you have to offer?" By our own example, we were meant to help them answer that question.[21]

I held back from following this script. In the six years I had passed at Harvard, physical therapy had restored some mobility to my left hand, particularly to my first finger, and I was able to play again, mostly simple chamber music, some movements from the Bach suites. Aided by the pain-free pleasures of the electric typewriter, I discovered I could write. It was enough; I was grateful for what I had. But there was no inspiring lesson for kids, I assumed, in such different circumstances.

On the positive side, it seemed important to stress the value of home—no one can make a solid new life through hatred of the past. So I talked about physical sensations which formed my memories of Chicago a quarter of a century before, small things like the faint whiff of cow dung which sometimes blew north to us from the Chicago stockyards, the clanging mechanical sounds of the factories nearer us.

The next speakers, sorted by age, came from various projects in Chicago. The stories these adults in their late thirties and early forties told about themselves might appear to a bourgeois audience too modest to be inspiring: a woman had learned shorthand and so become a secretary to a union official; a man managed to break into the electrical trades, one of the most racist in Chicago. The kids, however, listened respectfully: these were possible futures.

The person who spoke last was the youngest, a Puerto Rican man barely a decade out of the projects; he served as the *pièce de résistance*. His was indeed the most dramatic story: having kept away from the drug life of his contemporaries, he had gone to a local college, then a medical school, and was now a resident in eye surgery.[22]

The young doctor spoke with an evangelist's fervor about self-improvement. He began by telling about the pivotal moment in high school when he became a born-again Christian. He read out from notes he had kept about the daily stages of his spiritual rebirth and how it had altered his attitudes. When God spoke to him, he was far behind in science; he was obliged to start from scratch when he entered a local college. His message was entirely motivational; about his scientific education the young doctor said nothing.

In a way, it made good sense for him to omit discussing how he developed his talent. The message was that his young listeners had the power inside themselves to change themselves no matter what their talents. His religious invocation should have resonated, due to the supportive strength of ghetto churches. Moreover, the young doctor was no egoist holding himself up as a shining example; he had abandoned a pregnant girlfriend somewhere along the way.

But this mentor's speech made his audience angry, and they began heckling him. The inspiring story is, of course, in some ways always a provocation: "If I could do it, why can't you?" Moreover, in poor communities the adolescent possessor of ability is under pressure. You survive in a poor community not by being the best—or indeed the toughest—but rather through keeping your head down. Literally: you avoid eye contact on the street, which can be taken as a challenge; in school if you are gifted you try to render yourself invisible, so that you will not be beaten up for getting better marks than others.

Correspondingly, ghetto adolescents are highly sensitive to being "dissed," that is, dis-respected. In places where resources are scarce and approval from the outside world is lacking, social honor is fragile; it needs to be asserted each day. The young doctor certainly knew his brains constituted a provocation, he must have learned the art of survival through evasion and nonengagement, but now onstage he had raised his head. At our meeting, when a boy in the audience called out an obscenity the young surgery resident answered him back, though more politely: "You are not a victim! Strive!"

Our hosts became quite uneasy, fearing the verbal conflict would quickly become violent. But that was it. The young doctor persevered; the kids gradually lapsed into a sullen, hostile silence. At the end, the head community worker rose from her chair and thanked us without asking for general discussion.

I have no idea of what the community workers made of the event. My instant reaction was admiration of the young doctor's courage. But by now I was attuned enough to my more recent history to understand their anger. The young doctor spoke the language of an elite; he was the kind of student Harvard would have admitted with open arms. And this was because his was the language of potential, of a life project which he meant to fulfill. Whereas the language of the secretary and the electrician would be foreign at Harvard, even though it provided a guide to many young people about how to make something of themselves. Theirs was a language of small steps, of concrete, limited victories.

We like to believe that everyone has a talent of some kind, and that all abilities are worthwhile. Ability, however, takes two unequal forms. The particularities of doing something well fall within the circle of objective actions for which people are respected and respect themselves. Potential talent falls into a different category; it is a much more personal assessment, entwined with questions of motivation and will as much as of facility. Just this difference begets a profound inequality. The notion of transforming oneself supposes the power to leave behind the life one has known—which means leaving behind the people one has known. A "promising" individual like the young doctor could thus undermine the self-respect of those he had left behind. "If I could do it, why can't you?" is the message behind the command "Strive!" The young doctor had, to be sure, no cultural capital when he started out; his rise came solely within himself, and in his view from religious faith alone. But faith in his own future set him apart from his listeners. They, who were meant to be inspired, could not see far forward, or imagine another version of themselves; his self-confidence could only sharpen their sense of lack. Though he made them feel inferior, they did not suffer that feeling passively; they were tough kids, supersensitive to being "dissed."

I can understand from music why the secretary and electrician did not challenge the kid's sense of honor as the doctor did. Good music teachers shy away from discussing all a great piece of music possibly might contain, especially with beginners; precisely because of their physical incompetence, children cannot respond to the promise of possible expression. The good teacher wants to find a way to communicate directly and quickly with the student, and often finds the best way is through simple words like "faster," "ouch!" or "not bad." The point is to find a directive language which pupil and teacher can share, leading to action taken in small steps; in this, developing a musical gift is like a secretary learning stenography. Whereas the secretary showed the young people what to do, the young doctor told them who they should become.

In every social relationship we are at some point taken in hand by another person who guides us. The mentor's task is to present his or her own competence in such a way that the adult or child can learn from it. Just because competence is so elemental a component of self-worth, people who are meant to show their abilities as role models face a problem akin to the reserve of social workers: the fear of making an invidious comparison can mean they do not speak of their abilities. Not alluding to the touchy subject, however, not mentioning this divisive inequality, only makes the unspoken difference more important. In retrospect, it seems to me the young doctor would have done much better at our community meeting if he'd talked about learning science, even though his audience could probably not have followed what he was saying.

This incident was another revelatory scene for me, like the sudden awareness of my mother's work, though this time the curtain stayed up longer. I, too, was afraid of giving offense by pronouncing the word "Harvard." As soon as I left the community center, though, I knew I had made another kind of mistake. These kids, who could not define their own potential, who knew nothing about bourgeois propriety or security, had yet been forced beyond their years to learn everything about survival; they knew about limits. I should have spoken about the history of my hand; it would have made a real connection between us.

Interviewing

At Harvard, Riesman worried that I was brooding too much about my own problems. To lift me out of my emotional stew, both Riesman and Erikson suggested that I learn how to interview others.

In-depth interviewing is a distinctive, often frustrating craft. Unlike a pollster asking questions, the in-depth interviewer wants to probe the responses people give. To probe, the interviewer cannot be stonily impersonal; he or she has to give something of himself or herself in order to merit an open response. Yet the conversation lists in one direction; the point is not to talk the way friends do. The interviewer all too frequently finds that he or she has offended subjects, transgressing a line over which only friends or intimates can cross. The craft consists in calibrating social distances without making the subject feel like an insect under the microscope.

Erikson was wary of formalizing this craft, and by watching films of his work with young children I could see why; he seemed to enjoy playing with kids, all the while looking carefully at their every move—a clinician's version of what musicians call listening with the "third ear." In music, this experience is arduous but straightforward; a cellist corrects the sound as he or she makes it, for instance modulating pressure on the bow arm just after the sound is initiated to round it out. The "third ear" in interviewing, which requires that one stand both within and outside a relationship, is more mystifying because it lacks any physical measure. Erikson seemed to do it instinctively.

In the 1960s, though, other social scientists became self-conscious about the techniques of interviewing. By that decade, a perverse divide had come to separate the "hard" from the "soft" social sciences; people who dealt in numbers separated themselves from people who dealt in values, sentiments, and subjective understanding. The hard men dominated because they seemed to speak the language of fact. The humanists sought to defend themselves in part by arguing that much of what we know about social life is the result of interacting with other people; there are no "facts" free of our own engagement.

In anthropology, the humanistic view was cogently advanced by Clifford Geertz, who forced his colleagues to question their own role and presence in collecting information from foreign cultures. Among sociologists, this view was advanced and first applied specifically to interviewing in the 1930s and 1940s. The Polish sociologist Florian Znaniecki had created a school dedicated to gathering life histories; by the Second World War there were excellent social ethnographers in Sweden and Denmark; in America, before the war at the University of Chicago and after it at Berkeley, there were professors who hung out on the streets or haunted the corridors of mental hospitals—all sensitive to the difference their own presence made in the accounts they rendered.

As the divide widened in the 1960s between "hard" and "soft" social knowledge, ethnographic sociologists came to be more self-referential; whereas Erikson drew on his own experience to understand others, many of his followers used others to understand themselves. The larger culture of the Sixties, so touchy-feely, reinforced this self-referential emphasis.

Riesman, no less than Erikson, was an instinctive interviewer. He could ruin any cocktail party by transforming it into a group discussion; he handed money over to beggars on the street in exchange for their recent or not so recent histories; he frequently forgot to discuss the papers of students by interrogating them about what it meant, for instance, to be the eldest son of a Methodist minister from Kansas. But *The Lonely Crowd* is not an "inner-directed" book, to use its own principal term. Riesman is self-aware, yet disappears into his work.

The easiest way for me to cut my teeth as an interviewer, Riesman decided, would be to interview people in Boston's upper class. Himself the scion of a wealthy Jewish family in Philadelphia, Riesman had married into the WASP elite, a world he could treat with irony and without envy; about his station in society he had no anxiety. Looking back, I suspect he thought the interviews might make me more mannerly, as well as teach a skill. In any event, he immediately opened doors for me.

The "Boston Brahmins" were an elite which traced its origins back to the first European settlers in Boston, but really became powerful only with the growth of Boston as a port city in the late eighteenth century. By the middle of the nineteenth century, these New Englanders had created a tight network of banks, law firms, and stock brokerages which saw to the money. They had created their own private schools and dominated universities like Harvard. After the middle of the twentieth century, however, the polo ponies thinned out on the North Shore; Irish and Italian immigrants took away the Brahmins' long-lingering power in the city; Harvard succumbed to farmboy scientists and cosmopolitan Jews.

Americans of my background, it should be said, didn't quite treat people like the Boston Brahmins as class enemies. Of course we were against unearned privilege, but during the persecutions of the McCarthy era, the Bostonians and other American elites had proved largely immune to the mass anticommunist hysteria; their elders had often spoken out about civil liberties for leftists while middle-class liberals dithered.

Many were also patrons of concerts, like those at the Gardner Museum in Boston, concerts which had little social cachet. There was, at that time, a curious mingling of social worlds in music, the émigré Middle European world, represented by Serkin, and this old American culture, which had a long-ingrained habit of listening to music for pleasure. They mingled easily, for instance, at the summer festival Serkin ran in Marlboro, Vermont. But they did not merge or melt. By no stretch of the imagination can I imagine a Boston matron comfortably ensconced in a booth at the kosher deli; discussion of the relation between Art and Life would be more likely conducted in one of Boston's many churches.

The results of Riesman's opening various doors into this milieu were at first not auspicious. "My what, young man?" an elderly Boston matron replied when I asked her, point-blank over tea in the Somerset Club, to describe her identity. I had just made the tyro interviewer's error of assuming that frontal attack is the best way to elicit information from others. Nor did I do much better with a senior banker who declared, "I know just what you mean by 'identity.'" He patiently took me through his family's genealogy, courteously assuming, as we neared the present, that references to various living kin were to persons I had inevitably met.

"We go our separate ways," my matron replied when I asked about the working-class suburbs encroaching on their North Shore estates, and this brief statement sufficed. Boston's new money was treated with greater prejudice. In 1966, memories of the murdered President Kennedy were still fresh, his person sacrosanct. Still, the Irish-American president seemed to my informants not really "one of us," much as he appeared upper-class to other Americans. My subjects spoke freely about his father as "jumped up" and regaled me with stories about the family's misadventures in society.

In the freshness of youth, I concluded at first sighting that, in the corners of Boston remaining to them, the Brahmins had turned inward upon themselves, their sense of class honor static. Riesman pressed me to go back, and in doing so I saw that matters were indeed more complicated.

On returning to my matron, for instance, I found that she

was in dire straits financially and worked during the day selling cheap antiques in a shop. By any standard economic measure, she had become lower-middle-class. Her Brahminhood was an identity of the night, reassumed when she left work. She did not complain about this change of fortune. Indeed, she spoke with genuine pleasure in describing her deals with the suppliers and the buyers in the shop; that pleasure lay in a different compartment from the declaration "We go our separate ways."

The banker also had an identity of the night; in reinterviewing him I discovered, when he propositioned me, that he was gay. I rather regretfully declined, but must have done so tactfully; he unburdened himself of the traumas of a sexual life— Boston was still severely puritan—which if revealed would have spelled his social ruin. Yet his night life had modulated his day life. He liked finding "raw talent" and "house-training them" in the ways of his firm; undoubtedly there was a sexual overtone to this, but even so he was welcoming rather than snooty to outsiders.

Finally I interviewed Boston Brahmins who were my contemporaries, spending a few evenings at Harvard's Porcellian Club, a youthful Brahmin bastion in which people drank, ate, and occasionally read a book. Again, as with my banker, there was a lot of family gossip; families had known one another "forever," and their male children moved surefooted through a forest of obscure nicknames. When the talk turned serious about their future, however, they couldn't see forward. What they respected in their parents and in their ancestors no longer commanded the respect of others.

Diplomacy, for instance, once a refuge for the elite, was no longer theirs to command; their cultural impress was ever fainter. "Good manners" had become illegible to others; the habits of indirection and irony—their English side—did not register to our contemporaries, who were confrontational and declaratory. In chronicling the breakdown of "gentlemanly capitalism" in the City of London during the last twenty years, the banker Philip Augar is struck by how the traditional old-boy network has in fact given way to an equally clubby new-boy network, American and German bankers replacing the pin-striped locals in the City, still arranging corporate financing and jobs informally.[23] The members of the Porcellian Club had a premonition of this in Boston. The elite wouldn't disappear but the players would change; if they continued in the mold, these young men feared they would be dealt out.

All these interviewees conveyed a simple message: an elite can lose its prestige. But not simply. The Brahmins' lessened standing in the world did not diminish their mutual regard. Decline was something they managed, negotiated—just as the banker had negotiated his identity within the community. Like any other social attribute, respect is not a static quality, a fixed quantity. This truism takes on a peculiar life in interviews; indeed, the fluidity of interviewing reveals something important about the word "mutual" in the phrase "mutual respect."

An interviewer is meant to use his or her experience to understand others, rather than listen for echoes of his or her own life. More largely, common sense tells us that when others are treated as mirrors of oneself, they aren't accorded their own reality of their own existence; one has to respect the elemental fact that they differ. The lesson seems to be: if you respect them, don't project onto them.

Yet this is a very severe, a very puritanical lesson; indeed, it is forced and unnatural behavior. In everyday life we are constantly confusing self and other. As in interviewing, so in love, in parenting, and in work: it is by projection that we make a kind of elemental contact with others. That's what my banker did when he assumed, since he liked me, that I must have been born a Brahmin. I had an unwelcome shock of recognition in listening to the polite young men; an alarm had rung for them as it had for me—for the moment I forgot they were Brahmins. Adam Smith famously defined sympathy as often *falsely* imagining the pain of another as one's own.

In time, the confusion between self and other came to seem to me a vital clue in understanding what oils the gears of mutual respect. It begins as a mistake. That is, by making Adam Smith's "error" of mutual identification and so of sympathy, we overcome differences which stand in the way of working together. It's true that eventually, as in interviewing, we must recognize that what we have imagined about our spouses, children, or coworkers is not factually true. If either in interviewing or ordinary life we leave untreated the "mistake" of identification, we are caught in the toils of self-referential understanding; nothing outside ourselves is real. But confusion between self and other can also serve as a necessary point of departure for constructing a further social relationship, an evolving social bond.

In watching old films of Erikson playing with children, I now look at them somewhat differently than I did as a novice. To be sure, he is watching like a hawk what the children do, but it seems to me he can only do this because he too is enjoying building a dump truck out of building blocks. The children visibly enjoy his shared pleasure; they mistake him for one of themselves—and perhaps he too makes the "error" of imagining, for a moment, he is not an old man.

I had to understand the refusal to identify with others in the first truly independent work I did as an interviewer. I was now, in 1970, a young man with a grant. It permitted me and a colleague, Jonathan Cobb, to study the other end of the social scale in Boston: janitors, manual laborers, repairmen, and also women who worked as secretaries or clerks, the white-collar women often married to men who did manual labor. These were people who knew who they weren't: they weren't middle-class. No generous confusions of self and other among Boston's doctors, professors, or bankers had modified that fact.

To Europeans, America seems a mass rather than a class society, but gives this appearance only because class in America is hidden beneath a glossy surface of commercial culture. In the 1960s that glossy surface was broken as the white working classes turned on the professional classes, the liberal elite and its radical, countercultural children during the Vietnam War. They turned equally on poor blacks below, as parasites and welfare cheats. Right-wing politicians mobilized the resentment and class anger of this "silent majority"—though it seemed anything but silent.

The starting point of our interviews was that something other than right-wing belief fueled this class discontent.[24] We took about a hundred families, interviewing their members singly and in groups, our aim being to understand whether they had a distinctive consciousness of class and how it worked.

When we interviewed white workers alone, they spoke in a

balanced and open way about themselves in relation to others in the city. They were realistic about the tough times faced by poor blacks below them, and often quite funny about the pretensions of the vestigial Brahmins rather than resenting the elite. Stuck in low-status labors, they often felt they had failed in the task of making something of themselves through work. But they were not lacking in self-respect; this came to them through providing for their families. Middle-class people did not take much notice of that effort, however, and their indifference our interviewees treated as insulting.

When interviewed in groups, people switched off this balanced assessment of others and complex regard of self. They felt free to indulge in gross racial slurs and jokes, spurring one another on, railing against the liberal elite and the media, becoming the angry men and women manipulated by politicians. A zero-sum game of respect marked our group interviews—a game in which respect to blacks was denied in order to affirm one's own worth.

How to prevent this hostile, zero-sum game puzzled me thirty years ago, and it still does. Inequality had translated into a doubt of self; that doubt might be partly relieved by attacking the integrity of others—though I don't believe the attacks on blacks or liberals really made people feel good about themselves. Still, the condition of "not being seen" had produced a desire to avenge. Here, then, was one bleak result of the social scarcity of respect.

My childhood in Cabrini and the lives of these white workers form bookends to this problem, the inequalities of class and race clearly making it difficult for people to treat one another with respect. Within these bookends stand experiences harder to read: the need to hold back for the sake of respecting someone else, the divide between self-respect and group respect, the strength of self which diminishes others, the ill fit between self-confidence and the regard of others, the bond to others which results from the "error" of imagining you are alike. These may seem more subjective matters than life in a housing project or class rage, but social forces shape such personal experiences just as they shape the more "objective" conditions.

Chapter Two

What Respect Means

Nations go to war for the sake of their honor, labor negotiations run aground because the unions don't think management treats them with dignity, the courtiers of Louis XIV fought for whose prestige was great enough to sit on a stool in the presence of the king's nephew. Admiration is bestowed on a soldier who has fought bravely, firefighters feel pride in working together to put out a blaze, a scholar who has traced down an elusive fact finds satisfaction with his or her work. Respect seems so fundamental to our experience of social relations and self that we ought to define more clearly what it is.

Sociology has indeed many synonyms naming different aspects of "respect." These include "status," "prestige," "recognition," "honor," and "dignity." A list of these definitions would be dull, and they would remain mere abstractions; the social vocabulary of respect might be made to come to life, however, by returning to music.

When I first began to play chamber music, my teacher ordered me to respect the other players without, again, explaining what she meant. But musicians learn to do so, usually by using their ears rather than words. An illuminating instance of how this happens is furnished by two great musicians, the singer Dietrich Fischer-Dieskau and the pianist Gerald Moore, performing one of Schubert's most famous songs, "Der Erlkönig."[1] Were we backstage with them beforehand we could well imagine that they are a little nervous; this is also one of his most difficult lieder to make cohere.

Moore will have to perform a series of rapid, staccato notes and chords, like a machine gun firing; Moore's hands are certainly up to the task, but he has to worry about the volume. The piano should create a background of unrest as the singer pours out the story of a terrified child, of his father attempting to comfort him, and of the child's sudden, mysterious death. Moore can't play too loud, but Fischer-Dieskau must also help him, at moments when the child speaks, by reining in his own sound so that the terrifying effect of the staccato machine gun comes forward.

As in the many times he has performed "Der Erlkönig," Fischer-Dieskau rises to the challenge. Whereas singers bent on belting out their own part use the volume of the chest to produce the child's anguished cries, Fischer-Dieskau makes head tones, lifting the sound up to the top of his throat. And to reinforce the effect of the staccato piano chords, the singer takes a small liberty with the text in the middle of the song by more speaking than singing, and speaking harshly, just at a moment when Moore is playing such rich chords that their clanging effect could be lost. "Der Erlkönig" comes to its sudden, devastating end and the house goes wild.

The singer has respected the pianist's needs. It might be said that the collaboration succeeded thanks to the singer's own personality, but Fischer-Dieskau himself doesn't say this. In his writings, he plays down his own personal feelings, in part out of modesty, in part to argue against the cult of personality rife among singers, most of all because he believes performing strictly obeys the demands of the music itself.[2] His small liberty of the speaking voice came from what singer and pianist needed to do, together, at a particular moment to convey the dramatic sense of the music; it was no willful, idiosyncratic addition.

Fischer-Dieskau has taken the needs of Moore the pianist seriously, but Fischer-Dieskau's invocation of "Schubert" will alone hardly explain why; many performers of "Der Erlkönig" make a mess of the voice/piano texture. His talent? This answer leads into a thicket; we could hardly say that only exceptionally talented individuals are responsive to others. That's true neither onstage or off.

But Fischer-Dieskau's invocation of Schubert rather than himself is, however, helpful in one way. Imagine that the singer's willingness to pay attention to Moore, treating him as collaborator rather than accompanist, was indeed a question of personality, in particular how he felt about Gerald Moore as a man. Friendship would then have to precede their working relationship; conversely, the singer would have trouble performing with strangers. Moreover, Schubert is someone neither could know personally; the physical presence of the composer consists of line after line of inkblots. If the singer must attend to the needs of Gerald Moore's fingers, rather than to liking him, the talent of both men lies in their capacity to translate inkblots into feeling.

I make heavy weather of performing this song because it illuminates the sense of the words "taking the needs of others seriously" offstage, outside the concert hall.

The writer Michael Ignatieff has written that these others, in society, are mostly strangers.[3] We can know personally very few individuals; in complex societies a varied cast of social types crowds the scene, their lives not instantly comprehensible. What is in us, then, which responds to those whom we don't personally know? A little like Fischer-Dieskau, the sociologists C. Wright Mills and Hans Gerth answer it is a matter of character rather than personality, but they try to be more verbally explicit. "Character" to them means a person's communication with others through shared "social instruments"—the social analogues to the musical texts are laws, rituals, the media, codes of religious belief, political doctrines.

These texts, too, people perform rather than read: perform in court the law so that jurors are moved to acquit or convict, perform on the street, through eye contact or body language, the sentence "I will not hurt you." When people play these "social instruments" well they connect to strangers, become emotionally involved in impersonal events, engage themselves with institutions.

In their book *Character and Social Structure,* Gerth and Mills sought to apply this perhaps abstract formula to a dark reality offstage.[4] They puzzled over why a neurotic, confused individual might nonetheless withstand torture or protest injustices committed against others, whereas healthy, happy adults might prove cowards. Onstage, "Schubert" should invite only submission; offstage, the inquisitor's questions can elicit two opposite responses. The distinction between character and personality is a way to sort these out.

Many elements of personality go into suspension at testing moments of engagement with institutions; other elements come forward. Gerth and Mills believe that the neurotic who resists is strengthened by imagining other witnesses in the torture chamber to whom the victim signals when under the knife, expressing his commitment to these invisible comrades or to an abstract principle. It is such a capacity to engage the larger world which defines a person's character; character can be thought of, they say, as the relational side of personality, and transcends the dictum that only face-to-face relations are emotionally gripping.

The concert furnishes a positive example of character: treating with respect the need perceived in another when acting together. Character more largely conceived addresses the full range of society's inkblots; a person's character brings him or her to expressive life in human relations. The large view of character furnishes in turn a critical yardstick against which to measure other words in the vocabulary of "respect."

The first of these is "status." Status usually refers to where a person stands in a social hierarchy. In the concert hall, all that is needed to establish status is listing the singer in the program in larger type than the accompanist—the printing is all too often an accurate guide to what you will then hear. Society prints status in the same way and usually with the same consequence; it's the superior whose needs count and who gets recognition.

"Prestige" refers to the emotions which status arouses in others, but the relation between status and prestige is complicated. High status does not invariably dictate high prestige. A corrupt or bumbling aristocrat can lose prestige in the eyes of others while retaining his legal, privileged status; the person has, we say, demeaned his office. Prestige can also be detached from sheer rank. Research on occupational prestige shows, for instance, that people who do useful and independent craft-work, such as cabinetmakers, enjoy more prestige than elite business executives, wrapped up in corporate politics and not fully in control of their own labors. Finally, prestige can be transferred from persons to objects; a Porsche roadster is a prestigious item no matter who owns it.

Is "prestige" then a sufficient synonym for "respect"? Not quite: the doctor at our community meeting did work with much greater occupational prestige than the secretary—his work is both autonomous and socially useful—but she was treated with greater respect. Doing that prestigious work did not lead him to take seriously the specific need of his listeners for guidance. Again in the concert hall, Fischer-Dieskau's prestige, an admiration which he certainly earned, is constructed by us, his listeners; that audience construct doesn't explain his own attentiveness.

What's missing in these terms is something which conveys mutuality, which is what the word "recognition" does. The philosopher Fichte first cast recognition into legal language, exploring how laws can be framed so that the needs of strangers, foreigners, and migrants are acknowledged in a constitution. Rousseau enlarged the discussion of recognition to include the street as well as the court, mutual acknowledgment a matter of social behavior as much as of legal right. In the writings of John Rawls, recognition means respecting the needs of those who are unequal; in the writings of Jürgen Habermas, recognition means respecting the views of those whose interests lead them to disagree.

But the word "recognition," in these positive usages, is still not broad enough to encompass the awareness of mutual need. There is a further, and darker, element which consists of social honor. The word "honor" has an old-fashioned and rather Victorian ring, but in two ways is a much more fundamental category of social life.

Honor proposes, first, codes of conduct: a Bedouin tribesman obliged by custom to serve as guardian to his dead brother's children follows a code of honor. Second, honor signals a kind of erasure of social boundaries and distance. In the sociologist Pierre Bourdieu's words, honor supposes "an individual who sees himself always through the eyes of others, who has need of others for his existence, because the image he has of himself is indistinguishable from that presented to him by other people."[5] Both the strength and the perversity of social honor is to be found in mutuality of this sort.

In German National Socialism, the regime went to great lengths to make people feel that at last, after the humiliations of the past, they counted for something in each other's eyes—a perverse fulfillment of social honor. The affirmation of honor within a group, recognizing and responding to the needs of others, can lead to destructive behavior toward those who lie beyond the group's boundaries, as in the zero-sum game practiced by the Boston workers: to affirm the honor of our group, we have to denigrate the honor of yours.

The positives of recognition and the negatives of social honor define the poles of mutuality. Does self-respect fit between them? I've dwelt on my own experience as a musician to show why it may not. The craftsman—whether musician, cabinetmaker, or indeed executive when focused on the terms of a deal—concentrates on doing the job well, and this provides self-respect. Interpersonal relations, social process, mutuality, are not the point; the singer cannot just say to his partner, "I want to support you"; he has to know how.

Moreover, craftwork holds up a standard, hews to an ideal, which transcends sheer interpersonal process. Fischer-Dieskau, like most musicians, treats cooperation with his pianist as a means to another end, getting Schubert's inkblots right when translated into sound. Pursuit of this ideal standard ultimately yields the sense of self-respect: one got it right at last. The neurotic might have negotiated with his torturers, perhaps betraying just a few secrets; instead, he too wants to do the right thing. His character resides in aspiring to maintain an ideal, that of protecting other resisters; his self-respect depends upon it. While mutuality focuses on process, self-respect of this sort focuses on product.

So our musical example, which seemed so self-evident, leads to all sorts of complications offstage—just as it should. Status hardly fits, and prestige does not fit simply, into the character frame of respecting other people's needs. Recognition and the pursuit of social honor may breed that awareness, the latter at the cost of aggression against outsiders. Self-respect may be at odds with mutuality, because of the claims of both craftwork and conscience. There is one word left, and it is the most obscure.

The Kabyle of North Africa have a saying: "Man is man through men; God alone is God through himself."[6] The saying is meant in part to define a dignified human being: dignity comes through faith in God, no matter what the codes of honor, the communications among men, or the arts of expression.

Modern society has tried to find two secular equivalents of equal gravity.

One can be traced back to the first writers on universal human rights, notably the eighteenth-century jurist Cesare Beccarria. His work *On Crimes and Punishments* (1722) argues that torture for whatever reason, good or bad, defiles human dignity. It is an argument which posits that the body has natural boundaries of pain and pleasure. Fichte built his concept of human rights on respect for the integrity of the body, as Thomas Jefferson did also in the American Enlightenment. The act of respecting the pain of another is what confers on human beings a secular dignity akin in its gravity to respect in more traditional societies for the divine.

The other trajectory of modern secular society has been to emphasize the dignity of labor. The dignity of labor was a greatly foreign concept to ancient society, whose economy relied so greatly on slavery—though there are pastoral exceptions like Virgil's *Georgics*. Christian labor of the monastic sort was meant for the service of God, rather than dignified in itself. Guilds in the later Middle Ages occasionally subscribed to something like the self-sufficing dignity of labor; so too did families of specialized craftsmen like the Stradivarius violin makers. In the creation of the American Republic, the political analyst Judith Shklar argues, the value of hard work defined the ethos of the self-respecting citizen.[7] Still, Western society awaited the coming of modern capitalism for the idea of the dignity of labor to become a universal value.

The historians Linda Gordon and Nancy Fraser phrase that value as follows: "The worker tends to become the universal social subject: everyone is expected to 'work' and to be 'self-supporting.' Any adult not perceived as a worker shoulders a heavier burden of self-justification."[8] That element of "self-justification" is what Max Weber famously dissected. Weber's work ethic is about man or woman "proving" himself or herself through work; what the individual is proving is his or her basic worth; to Weber, the proofs offered are petty scrimpings and savings, the denial to oneself of pleasures, exercises of self-control—a kind of moral fitness training through work.

Many commentators dispute Weber's description of the work ethic; consumption is missing from it, as is any idea of work satisfaction—the pleasures and dignity of craft. But few critics would dispute the social frame into which Weber set the work ethic. The work ethic is competitive, requires comparative judgments of worth; those who win may turn a blind eye to those who lose.

The dignity of the body thus differs from the dignity of work, when labor takes this form. Both are universal values: the dignity of the body is a value all people can share; the dignity of work only a few can achieve. While society may respect the equal dignity of all human bodies, the dignity of labor leads in quite a different direction: a universal value with highly unequal consequences. Invoking dignity as a "universal value," moreover, provides in itself no clue about how to practice an inclusive mutual respect.

These contrary concepts return to the stage, where the singer treats the pianist as his equal. Offstage, practices of status, prestige, and social honor do not incline toward equality; the craftsman's self-respect is indifferent to it. We might address these limits by trying to make society more resemble the concert; that is, by exploring ways to perform as equals, and so show mutual respect.

The musical example makes clear, however, just how difficult this would be. Part of what makes both men rare performers is that they have *achieved* mutuality; many musicians have the cooperative impulse, but few manage to translate it into sound. Even more so is this true of social life; an enormous gap exists between wanting to act well toward others and doing so.

Radical egalitarians have sometimes argued that if material conditions can be equalized, then mutually respectful behavior will spring forward, "naturally" and spontaneously. This expectation is psychologically naive. Even if all unjust inequalities could be removed in society, people would still face the problem of how to shape their worse and their better impulses. I don't suggest accepting or accommodating inequality; rather, I argue that in social life as in art, mutuality requires expressive work. It must be enacted, performed.

The ambiguity of character introduces a further complication: if character is that element of subjective life which pays close attention to the social text, yet the vagaries of personal character lead people to their own separate interpretations. The command "Respect others!" could not simply be obeyed by following a strict, single set of rules; subjective desire governs the willingness to obey, and the manner in which people might respond.

In sum, if behavior which expresses respect is often scant and unequally distributed in society, what respect itself means is both socially and psychologically complex. As a result, the acts which convey respect—the acts of acknowledging others—are demanding, and obscure.

Part Two

An Inquest on Respect

Society shapes character in three ways so that people earn, or fail to arouse, respect.

The first way occurs through self-development, particularly through developing abilities and skills. The highly intelligent person who wastes a talent does not command respect; someone less gifted working to the limits of his or her ability does. Self-development becomes a source of social esteem just because society itself condemns waste, putting a premium on efficient use of resources in personal experience as much as in the economy.

The second way lies in care of the self. In the ancient world, taking care of oneself meant learning how to regulate the body's pleasures and pains; St. Augustine believed Man cares for himself by learning how to admit sin to God; Machiavelli thought taking care of oneself synonymous with protecting oneself, through arousing fear or awe in others. Care of oneself can mean additionally not becoming a burden upon others, so that the needy adult incurs shame, the self-sufficient person earns respect. This way of earning respect derives from modern society's hatred of parasitism; if society fears waste, it even more fears—whether rationally or irrationally—being sucked dry by unjustified demands.

The third way to earn respect is to give back to others. This is perhaps the most universal, timeless, and deepest source of esteem for one's character. As though watching a play, we might applaud brilliance or displays of ability; Machiavelli's prince might arouse the homage of submission, but neither the virtuoso nor the tyrant touches the sentiments of others as does someone who gives something back to the community. Nor is self-sufficiency enough to earn this kind of esteem; the self-sufficient person is ultimately of no great consequence to other people, since he has no mutual connection, no necessary need of them. Exchange is the social principle which animates the character of someone who gives back to a community.

Inequality plays a particular and decisive role in shaping these three character types. The unusual person who makes full use of his or her abilities can serve as a social icon, justifying inadequate provision of resources or regard for people who are not developing as fully; the celebration of self-sufficiency and fear of parasitism can serve as a way of denying the facts of social need; the compassion which lies behind the desire to give back can be deformed by social conditions into pity for the weak, pity which the receiver experiences as contempt.

The exploration of how inequality affects character I intend as an inquest, the word "inquest" suggesting an impartial inquiry. I've tried to discipline myself to that end by asking how much and in what ways inequalities are inescapable facts of social life. But also, it should be said, like a juror I do not bring to this inquiry an entirely unbiased mind.

Chapter Three

Unequal
Talent

Early in 1974 I flew to London for a celebration. Murray Perahia had won the Leeds Piano Competition—a big event in the musical world; cash, concerts, and recordings followed in its wake—and one of the sponsors gave the celebration party in her home.

In New York, an event like this would be as much a celebration of the money behind the competition as of the winner himself, a scene framed by waiters in black tie and filled by women in chic black sheaths refusing an endless round of elaborate canapés. In the London house, young women university students opened the door and served; an elderly lady clutching an enormous tumbler of whisky in one hand and a stack of disgusting white-bread sandwiches in the other loomed up, announced to me, "I always get gas on airplanes," and handed me the plate—an odd introduction to a royal personage.

She had in tow one of the judges of the competition. A pianist who'd begun her own career by winning a big prize in Eastern Europe, this elderly musician had served on many juries since, but reluctantly. "I don't believe in artists competing," she said, "yet it's the only way to find them." She was obliged to discuss and argue with the other judges, and she had to justify her decisions in committee, which seemed absurdly bureaucratic. She particularly disliked the guessing game of whether a young contestant had the potential to develop. The confident ones usually made a display of their technique but held back from taking artistic risks, so you just couldn't know what lay on the horizon of possibilities.

This was, as I argued with her, hardly the case with Murray Perahia; though his technique was even then entirely assured, it wasn't what you listened to in his playing. She then told me something nice about him. He listened quietly to the other contestants, occasionally fingering along with the performer. In too many competitions that I'd observed, the musicians behaved like athletes, aggressive toward other contestants, often putting down their efforts.

The bonhomie of this occasion indeed contrasted to a cello competition I myself had judged the year before. After this earlier event, there had also been a party, to which the hostess had invited the losing players, as a kindly gesture. The young woman who won the cello contest tried to mix with the others, but they held aloof. They gathered in little knots, going over what each thought were mistakes he or she had made, trying to assay what had gone wrong; for the moment, at least, there would be few thoughts of taking risks, of exploring artistic horizons; the competition had paralyzed them.

As the evening ended, our hostess made a small speech. She addressed herself to the losing players, saying it was a pleasure to hear all of them; they should look at the event as a point of departure in their careers. The warmth in her voice brought wan smiles in response, but they didn't seem convinced. The consolation party was perhaps cruel just because it was, despite good intentions, a lie. How could the young cellists who attended treat the contest as if it didn't matter?

Music competitions, as the Leeds judge remarked, may display inequalities of talent in such a way as to inhibit the development of expression; they may challenge the self-confidence of all but one of the participating musicians. The answer to these undoubted ills would be a less competitive view of talents— talent treated as one kind of difference among many, each person gifted in his or her own way. At our consolation party, the hostess wanted to convey something like this, but, as I say, the young cellists could not bring themselves to believe her.

The Respect Owed to Talent

The Leeds Piano Competition embodies in the artistic sphere a desire which has deep roots in modern society, that of making careers open to talent. No matter where the young pianists come from or who their parents are, anyone can apply; the sole criterion for reward is one's own personal ability. Such rules seem to us self-evidently just but would have appeared novelties to our ancestors.

In the *ancien régime* most posts in government, the army, or the church were inherited. The duc de Saint-Simon records in 1722, for example, a baby who becomes captain of the vast body of Swiss Guards in France, a post "the father had already inherited from the grandfather."[1] Saint-Simon is an aristocrat of the old school in finding nothing amiss here. Sheer talent counted for little in handing out privileges; ability had little to do with hierarchy.

Blindness to talent especially ruled abilities of an economic sort. Before the seventeenth century, business skills were mostly associated with the pariah Jews, whose supposed talent at making money elicited contempt. In Shakespeare's *Merchant of Venice*, the good Christians are business incompetents. That's part of what makes them gentlemen. Something more than prejudice explains this blindness. The money economy was primitive; barter of goods was more frequent than cash exchange; the calculation of risks was a game only mathematical savants could play; modern practices like double-entry bookkeeping seemed arcane arts on a par with alchemy.

The seventeenth-century English diarist Samuel Pepys embodied a great change in the relations of individuals to the social order; his career staked out the claim that individuals are owed respect because of their unique talents, a claim which made him superior to Shakespeare's economically incompetent gentlemen.

Pepys was a gifted government official, working mostly in the Admiralty; he valued his own practical capacities more than what we value him for—his art as a writer. Though hardly a man sprung from the masses, he made his way in the Admiralty by being particularly good at his work. Of course Pepys was armed with all the skills of the classic courtier; he knew how to flatter and toady, how to effectively stab his colleagues in the back. But his claim to individual privilege came from his ability to count.

On April 8, 1664, for instance, we find him throwing his weight around with the contractor of "poop lanterns" for the boats of the Admiralty, Pepys having calculated their true value and so determined to break the contract the government had entered into; the contractor, Pepys says, "will come to reason when I can make him to understand [the numbers.]"[2] Getting the numbers right will earn him, he hopes, particular respect from his superiors. On the 22nd of December, 1665, we find him figuring out a new system of government accounts, one his superiors do not quite understand; again Pepys explains, in the spirit of a master rather than a servant.

The phrase "careers open to talent" came into common currency in Pepys's generation, in the mid-seventeenth century, and mostly among people of Pepys's station. Politically, they argued for a well-run state which made room for "new men" of bourgeois origins, particularly in the administration of finance; money was too important to leave in the hands of aristocrats.

From the later Middle Ages on, the church and the legal profession had indeed made room for "new men," but it was room of a different kind. The church hierarchy had long been an avenue to power. Theological finesse was hardly required to travel this route; family relations or simple intrigue counted for much more. Many of the religiously gifted, moreover, following Christian precept, eschewed worldly power.

The legal profession certainly recognized talent, and that talent translated into a claim for privilege. At the end of the Middle Ages, in about 1470, Sir John Fortesque codified that claim as follows:

> . . . just as the head of the body physical is unable to change its nerves or to deny its members proper strength and due nourishment of blood, so a king who is the head of the body politic

is unable to change the laws of that body, or to deprive that same people of their own substance uninvited or against their wills.[3]

If lawyers worked as servants of the state, their skills and understanding would make them also the judges of their masters. Pepys asserts, however, the superiority of financial reckoning over the contractual power of words, and indeed the possession of quantitative skills gave a new meaning to the talent in the phrase "careers open to talent."

Legal ability in Pepys's day required a prodigious memory, in order to quote precedent. Quantitative skill appeared to adhere in the individual as a distinctive personal gift, the ability to calculate for oneself not dependent on the calculations of others; in 1664, Pepys will not accept the official numbers for poop lanterns as authoritative, just because they are legal. "Careers open to talent" meant that the talented individual had the right to show what he or she could do on his or her own; in 1665, Pepys shows his superiors what they do not understand, even though they are his superiors. A century later, the Physiocrats—a group of British and French accountants and financiers—would assert that the official accounts kept by states were no more than suspicious records to be subjected to constant scrutiny by an elite of mathematical brains.

But both lawyers and accountants, from Pepys's time onward, united in asserting that privilege should be *earned*, and that ability was the coinage of these earnings. Not surprisingly, titled aristocrats resisted that claim; so did the central state. Individual ability was an inner power which royal authority could not easily control. In the court of Louis XIV, Saint-Simon therefore reports, "The King was in the habit of filling high posts with men of no [titled] account so that he might, if the fancy took him, dismiss them as he would a valet."[4] The men treated like valets in fact were *robins*, at the top of the bourgeoisie. In the Age of the Sun King, new men were subject to ridicule if they overtly sought the trappings of elite honor; they had to insinuate themselves deviously. By the end of the reign of Louis XV, however, the mask of servility was more frequently removed.

"Careers open to talent" had become a doctrine enlarged from the realm of state offices to a more sweeping sociological principle, that of "natural aristocracy." Jefferson, for one, aimed at replacing "an artificial aristocracy founded on wealth and birth" by "a natural aristocracy . . . of worth and genius [to be] sought out from every condition of life."[5] Like the French Physiocrats, Jefferson meant to achieve this by a general change in institutions.

The Leeds Piano Competition embodies just the kind of institution these new men had in mind when they imagined a career open to talent. We might in turn imagine the portrait of a talented individual framed on four sides by institutions. On the left side of the frame, institutional reformers established regular competitions for posts. On the right side, they created institutions to train those who would take the exams; here lay the origins of specialized military academies and technical schools—and musical conservatories. On top, there had to be some objective measure of achievement; there needed to be an institutional standard equivalent to musical technique. In Physiocratic statecraft, this was created by use of accounting regimes like double-entry bookkeeping, which made it possible to know factually how well a bureau or bureaucrat managed the relation between income and expense.[6]

The bottom of this institutional frame, supporting the structure as a whole, was the most contentious: there needed to be ways of institutionalizing failure. You couldn't reject an inspector of finances on a whim; as on the judges at Leeds, there was pressure on you to explain and justify your rejection.

Abrupt, arbitrary dismissal had long been the rule of most monarchical regimes. In the seventeenth century, Henry VIII had kept his most talented servants in a state of terror by suddenly, for no apparent reason, sending one or another to the Tower or the executioner's block. The reformers reasoned that rewards for ability could not be given without corresponding acts of defining and punishing incompetence.

In retrospect, it may seem neither logical nor necessary to propose that for every winner there must be a loser, which is the principle of a zero-sum game. But the reformers had a kind of character-building purpose in mind. If dismissal was based on rational rules, bureaucrats would be forced to take more personal responsibility for their offices. Louis XIV's landscape architect, Le Nôtre, the creator of the Versailles gardens, charmingly observed that if a tree was out of place, "it is not the tree's fault but mine." Failure in office reflected back on the individual. This merging of rational rules and personal judgment reached an apotheosis of sorts a century later in the trials of Warren Hastings in the 1780s. Hastings, a corrupt and brutal official in the East India Company, was attacked by Richard Brinsley Sheridan and Edmund Burke in Parliament, the proceedings followed avidly by the public. The most striking thing about Sheridan's rhetoric is that it fused Hastings's immoral and worthless character to his incompetence; few of Pepys's contemporaries would have made such a connection. Now, because Hastings failed the test of ability, his career seemed illegitimate—though he managed to hold on to it.[7]

Surviving guild records from the Middle Ages show that the talents of individual bakers or weavers earned a local respect. Renaissance princes honored talented artists. The modern difference is the erection of a more generalized bureaucracy of talent; the extension of this bureaucracy into realms where earlier ages expected inherited privilege to rule; and judgments rendered on personal character based on individual fitness and competence.

One result of creating this modern institutional picture frame was that "talent" increasingly appeared a phenomenon which could be put on formal, public display. Exam results and accounts were published, dismissal for cause explained, exposed. The display of talent became a kind of performance— literally so during the course of the eighteenth century. Bureaucratic talent came to seem not so far removed from other kinds of performing ability.

At the beginning of the eighteenth century, for instance, "virtuoso" named someone with diverse interests, equally absorbed by old paintings, the improvement of farming, and innovations in wigs—a man or woman of many parts, an amateur. By the beginning of the nineteenth century, "virtuoso" referred to someone with a specialized skill displayed on stage to a dazzled public. Horace Walpole was a virtuoso of the old sort, the violinist Paganini a virtuoso of the new.

Virtuosity of this new sort widened the gulf between performer and public. The amateur could never hope to play the violin like Paganini, nor reckon sums like that ace Physiocrat Jacques Necker. Moreover, the audience could never hope to understand how the virtuoso accomplished his or her feats. This wonderment in the arts became in professional life a source of domination; professional violinists have their parallel in the nineteenth-century doctors whose expertise did not resemble that of the old barber-surgeons, a skill readily understandable to the person shaved or, equally, cut. Rather than having more of the skills understandable in everyday life, the master had a different kind of skill, unfathomable—a difference in kind rather than in degree of ability. From that difference came an ever-increasing inequality. Because his skills could not be understood, those over whom he held sway could only be his spectators, his subjects.

If, that is, we think of specialized talent just in terms of technique, we miss an important element of its sociology. In its evolution, specialized talent propounded a mystery, that of the professional, the virtuoso whose ability was hard for others to fathom. The careers open to talent became increasingly bureaucratized, rationalized; skill itself became increasingly a public enigma. To be sure, Pepys's contemporaries could no more write out a formula for how to become a great accountant than we can for how to become a musician of Perahia's stature; the difference, again, lies in institutions. Modern society has developed bureaucratic formulas for how to reward the endowments of ability, how to give talent its due: the Leeds Piano Competition is one such formula for rewarding the mystery contained in Perahia's hands.

The enigma of talent has taken on a second twist in contemporary society, seemingly just the opposite of specialized skill.

This is concern for potential ability as opposed to actual achievement. The piano judge doubted she could discover potential ability through a musical competition; indeed, she feared the competition would freeze the contestants, penalize them for taking risks. But what kind of ability is this, an ability as yet unrealized, put at risk by the formulas of competition in society?

Potential Ability

The entrance exams for French military academies in 1782 posed what to modern eyes look like quite sophisticated problems in geometry. The examiners set these problems, however, in very simple verbal terms, trying to eliminate the privilege of any prior education in mathematics. They were trying, as we would say, to eliminate "cultural bias," to discover potentially talented individuals among a mass of people who lacked social advantages. But the exam was not an exercise in equalization of social groups; it aimed at lifting unusual individuals out of the mass—more, it assumed these future officers already had developed the power in themselves to reckon and to strategize, an existent ability the examiners could pick up if only the issues involved were put to the youngsters in the right way.

Modern proponents of affirmative action in education or in jobs take a different tack. Like the eighteenth-century military examiners, they assume that social inequalities and privileges hold people back—but what is held back in the eyes of the modern reformer is germinating ability which people may not know they possess and could develop. In turn, that logic suggests that if we promote groups of people to a more encouraging setting, they may flourish as a group. Institutional acceptance has therefore to precede the measurement of ability. This logic breaks the formal relation between the top and the bottom of the old bureaucratic frame; rewarding talent does not entail naming and rejecting those who show, as yet, no equal evidence of it.

American data evinced by William Bowen and Derek Bok, based on racial preferences in universities, strongly suggest that groups do flourish when the old frame is broken, but both the data and the justice of this policy have been contested; group preferences based on what someone might become seem unfair to what other individuals have "earned" by their existent, measurable abilities.[8] Yet, in the long history of social practices, affirmative action poses a different question about the enigma of talent, about ability which might exist but not yet.

One of the cognomens for potential ability is the ugly word "aptitude," but it is also a revealing coinage. It elides being good or "apt" at something to one's "attitude." Affirmative-action policies are all about aptitude in this sense; they link the ability to learn to attitudes which stimulate the desire to achieve rather than erode belief in oneself. A generation ago, a group of researchers directed by the psychologist David McClelland sought to analyze the elision of apt and attitude which produces aptitude. McClelland argued that all humans possess "achievement motivation," the urge to do any task well.[9] He claimed even more radically that this desire controls any rational or cognitive activity—a radical claim because it proposes that belief in oneself precedes the ability to learn, reversing Descartes's famous dictum so that it would read *Sum ergo cogito*.

As other researchers were to discover, this formula could prove both depressing and disturbing to the subjects to whom it was applied. McClelland's formula suggests that if people are failing to learn, they must lack motivational will or desire. Clinicians working with poor achievers discovered that since the formula plays down the content of knowledge, it becomes almost perversely difficult to relieve self-blame if the under-achiever is not learning: "Something must be wrong with me"—but that "something" is hard to define.

The ambiguous relation between character and potential ability often also troubles those who benefit from affirmative-action policies, as Bowen and Bok themselves admit: "Do I personally deserve this opportunity, have I been given a chance only because of my race?" Such questions are likely to throw the young person back on the issue of achievement motivation rather than focus the mind on learning.

Stressing the link between potential ability and motivation can have an equally depressing effect in the workplace. "In the corporate world hierarchies of roles have been replaced," writes one exponent of the motivational school, "by . . . work in which the 'person' is as important as the technical skills they may possess; indeed the two have become inseparable."[10] Modern organizations judge the "whole man," and especially what the whole man might become. In work as in education, the bald judgment "You have little potential" is devastating in a way "You have made a mistake" is not.

At our meeting in Chicago, the young people were promised in the most elemental way a career open to talent; role models were there to assure them it was possible. They had perhaps no choice but to believe us; remaining as they were they would perish. If I try to imagine the community meeting taking place today, the opaque meaning of "potential ability" would, I think, be the driving issue. The electrician and the secretary represent a practicable model of competence, while the doctor projected an image of what one should become but offered no clue about how to become it.

The ambiguities of potential in a competitive society shaped the worry of the piano judge—the devastating implications of rendering judgment on someone's future, on someone's potential to develop as a human being.

Here then is an enigma of talent opposite from but equal to that of the virtuoso or brain surgeon whose talent is a mystery to others: a potential which is a mystery to oneself. The villain lurking in aptitude is the concept of potential itself, which issues a promise, if only the individual has the desire, but does not specify what the promise consists of.

Aptitude would have been a nonsensical concept to Pepys. What mattered to him was simply what you know how to do. But he would have found equally strange the modern work world, in which aptitude plays an ever more important role in shaping careers.

During the Industrial Revolution, the doctrine of careers open to talent made headway faster within government bureaucracies and in the professions than in the realms of manufacturing and commerce. As Adam Smith was the first to note, the division of labor in manufacturing meant that a carpenter who made an entire cabinet could be replaced in the manufacturing process by unskilled workers who did only one small part of the total job—more efficient in producing cabinets in large numbers but "deskilling" a traditional craft. The same process of deskilling often marked the white-collar world; the advent of the mechanical typewriter, for instance, transformed the status of clerks so that many were henceforward confined to the single task of typing, while others did equally specialized routine jobs.

Before the last century, in the higher reaches of the business world, few managers or owners justified their positions in terms of superior intelligence. For every Andrew Carnegie who emphasized rational management skills, there were many more Jay Goulds advocating sheer aggression and driving greed as the secret of business success. "Aptitude" meant simply a taste for competitive combat. Few businesses, moreover, had the structural frame which characterized the bureaucratic state: business schools hardly existed in the nineteenth century, jobs were not won by sitting for exams, nor did private enterprise develop the same objective criteria for defining failure as did government.

A generation ago, the sociologists Daniel Bell and Alain Touraine independently argued that modern commerce was about to catch up to the changes which had been brewing so long in the state and in the professions. The last third of the twentieth century, they said, would see a dramatic turn from an industrial to a postindustrial society, a turn in which the doctrine of "careers open to talent" would finally triumph. Knowledge-based work would become more economically significant than manual labor or routine jobs. Rough manufacturing and repetitive service work would be done by machines; human beings would instead do more mental service, technical, and communications work.

Neither could foresee quite how profitable it would become to export routine, manual labor to the Third World, instead of replacing human beings by high-tech and expensive machines nearer to home. But Bell and Touraine were prescient about the ever-increasing value placed on skill itself, and the inequality between elite and mass the possession of skill would generate. The economist Robert Reich, among others, points to the emergence of a "two-tier" society in North America, Western Europe, and Japan, based on control of knowledge, widening the income and wealth distance between the middle classes and the top.[11] Development economists point to the emergence in countries like India, Israel, and the Philippines of skills elites that form a kind of parallel stratum to the traditional top classes.[12]

But still these are definable, often highly technical skills. The society which Bell and Touraine announced also has need of another kind of skill, less fixed, more mobile, more adaptable. New forms of work require people who are good at moving from task to task, job to job, place to place. In part this is due to shifting demand in the global marketplace; organizations must change their functions, business plans, and products on short notice. The ability to learn new things quickly becomes then of more value than the capacity to go ever deeper into an existing problem or body of data. And, since such an ability is worth more than fixed knowledge, the potential for learning is more serviceable than past achievement. This is the economic premium put on "potential ability."

The examiners for entrance to the military academies in 1782 wanted to present to candidates problems couched in the most familiar terms. Modern aptitude tests do also, but also want to explore a child's powers of interpretation when confronted with new and unfamiliar material. The attitude tested by aptitude tests is just that willingness to analyze something new; economic utility lies in that capacity. For the same reason, elite business schools in America now favor students with non-commercial preparations, the ability to learn a language, for instance, seeming to token an adaptive mind.

Generalized intelligence tests, it should be stressed, are themselves quite ambiguous predictors of future success in either school or work. The American sociologist Christopher Jencks estimates that IQ tests given in early adolescence will explain 30–40 percent of the variation in years of school completed, 20–25 percent of the variance in occupational status in a randomly selected year, and more finely, 10–15 percent of the variance in annual earnings for workers between the ages of thirty and forty.[13] That is, single-number measures of intelligence explain some of the inequalities in schooling or work, but not much. Family background, class, personal motivation, and sheer luck count together for more in shaping the future.

Still, Nicholas Lemann, an analyst of aptitude tests, doesn't doubt they measure something real. What worries him is the uses made of such tests; they minimize local and particular achievements gained through plodding effort, emphasizing instead something yet to come. Worse, they move ever earlier into the life cycle an assessment of the possibilities which will be subsequently open to adults.

Assessments of aptitude increasingly make of childhood the primal scene of social inequalities—taken to an extreme in Britain and America in parents worrying about getting their toddlers into the right nursery schools. The armies of assessors become interpreters of childhood, looking, for instance, at what signs of aptitude appear in the ways children play. By contrast, the primal scene of inequality for Pepys was adulthood, and the measure of ability only what adults knew of one another's behavior. The assessment of people too young to be judged is also, I think, what was really on the mind of the elderly pianist at the Leeds Competition—expressed by her as the desire to set potential ability free, rather than paralyze a young artist prematurely.

In sum, the claim of a just reward for ability began as a revolt against privilege determined by inherited position. Modern society learned gradually how to construct institutions which framed talent. But the talents framed were increasingly mysterious—to others in the case of virtuoso or highly technical skills, to oneself in the case of aptitude and potential ability. This enigma was not benign. The specialist wielded powers over others they did not understand; the emphasis on aptitude and potential has shoved ever earlier into the life cycle the judgment of what reward should be given to individuals for their abilities.

None of this history, it could be objected, necessarily implies a problem of self-respect or mutual respect. The cellists at the party who didn't win may well recover and go on to lead satisfying lives, just as our hostess hoped. The young black who has been socially promoted through an affirmative-action program may nourish a love of learning for its own sake. And even, it might be said, the children who do not show aptitude in nursery school are not consigned to a dark fate—at least, tests of their abilities are not implacable predictors of their future. Put largely, the inequality of talents may be only one, limited element in determining the practices of respect.

To understand why this benign view of the relation between

ability and respect is not realistic, we need to dig a little more deeply into the phenomenon of ability itself, as it shapes the sense of character.

Two Character Types

Ability can be put in the service of craft, or it can be put in the service of mastery over others. Craft concerns the capacity to make a thing well; mastery concerns the demonstration to others of how well something is made. The craftsman and the master represent two character types; they elicit respect in two very different forms.

The distinction between craft and mastery is sharply defined in a poem of W. H. Auden's, "Sext," the third part of the *Horae Canonicae*, written in 1954. Auden evokes the capacities of the craftsman as follows:

> You need not see what someone is doing
> to know if it is his vocation,
>
> you have only to watch his eyes:
> a cook mixing a sauce, a surgeon
>
> making a primary incision,
> a clerk completing a bill of lading,
>
> wear the same rapt expression,
> forgetting themselves in a function.

He immediately in "Sext" contrasts to the craftsman's strength the ability to demonstrate superiority:

You need not hear what orders he is giving
to know if someone has authority,

you have only to watch his mouth:
when a besieging general sees

a city wall breach by his troops,
. . . when,

from a glance at the jury, the prosecutor
knows the defendant will hang,

their lips and the lines around them
relax, assuming an expression

not of simple pleasure at getting
their own sweet way but of satisfaction

at being right. . . .[14]

The sense of craft requires investment in the object of one's labor as an end in itself: as Auden says in his poem, forgetting oneself in a function. Whereas in mastery the object is a means to another end, that of displaying what you have done, what you have become, to another. Showing off mastery requires in part the approval of others, but it also is a self-conscious satisfaction, the "satisfaction at being right."

When Auden speaks of forgetting oneself in a function, the function itself is hardly mechanical. Just as the qualities of individual instruments differ, for instance, so do musicians' bodies; for the cello, differences in palm shape and finger length dictate differing positioning of the left hand on the strings in order to achieve correct pitch. Developing a craft-ability requires focusing on that zone of activity where rules encounter resistance or anomalies; it is exploratory work.

A computer programmer can, as a craftsman, be absorbed in the problems and glitches of a program; as a master, he or she will want to emphasize its advantages in comparison to other programs. An equally important difference between craft and mastery concerns time. Craftwork is slow: it accumulates step by step, it requires practice. Whereas the act of displaying one's mastery can take only a few moments; in our community meeting, the young doctor's display of mastery required but a few sentences to show, as in Auden's poem, that he was "right."

Putting the matter this way, the practice of craft may seem an inherently more worthy activity than the effort to demonstrate mastery. But I hope the reader will have drawn from my memoir the same lesson that I drew from doing musical craftwork: it is not character-forming in relation to other people.

Part of the reason is simply that the "ability" of craft labor lies in one's capacity to obsess about details; a psychoanalyst might say the craftsman is ruled by object compulsion. In music, learning to play in tune, achieving accuracy of pitch, is an obsessional concern occupying most string musicians for years of their training. But just this obsession means that craftwork can focus on things to the exclusion of focusing on other people—which was certainly true of me as a young musician.

There is a more complicated way in which craftwork is not character-forming. In the performing arts it concerns the fealty that any performer, whether great like Fischer-Dieskau or just a garden-variety singer, may feel toward a musical text. The text is its own reality; we relate ourselves to it, not it to us. An actor in *The Cherry Orchard* is meant to bring Chekhov's doctor to life, rather than use it as a report on his own recent experience of surgery. But for just this reason, craft labor can easily lead to dissociation from other human beings, as well as to standing back from oneself.

The failures of character which attend craftwork are those of indifference. It appears often when professional musicians listen to amateurs who play out of tune—or rather, they stop listening, not paying attention to whatever else the amateur might be doing. In compromising pitch the amateur has traduced the standards of craft. Attention, let alone mutual respect, comes only for those who have made the effort, engaged the difficulties of doing it right. Similarly, within the inward-turning realm of craft labor, whatever the sloppy or careless worker thinks about you doesn't count for much in your own sense of self.

Because of these exigencies, craftwork can fail to fit easily into the open, welcoming, mutually adjusting territory of a socially responsive character. Craftwork, the sociologist Thorstein Veblen argued, provides self-respect; to which needs be added, but not necessarily mutual respect.

Self-respect founded on craft embodies the claims to legitimacy which first animated the proponents of careers open to talent, just as it is the kind of ability Thomas Jefferson and Physiocrats like Jacques Necker imagined as that possessed by a natural aristocracy. The focus is first and foremost on the quality of work. Moreover, craft labor is individuating; no rule alone, no teacher, can do this work for someone else. But craftwork is the very antithesis of ability understood as a potential, as a possibility; neither intentions nor intimations count, only results. In the testing situation, exploring all the difficulties contained in a problem embodies the craft spirit, but this would prove disastrous to the test-taker. So craftsmanship is, as Veblen said, a very old-fashioned virtue, though it is not a sociable virtue.[15]

Mastery falls in the terrain of social honor. If displaying one's abilities to others were merely an effort to dominate or to win praise, then this show of ability would be nothing more than a bid for prestige. But displays of mastery are not so simple; they can also be motivated by the effort to teach others, to mentor them. By showing the kids at our community meeting how she learned stenography, for instance, the secretary served as a master to them. She explained an embodied code of conduct—an essential ingredient of social honor—and did so to address their own lack of knowledge of what to do.

On the positive, character-affirming side of social honor, a person makes a display of strength in order that another person may imitate it. But just here lies also a great problem: the person trying to respond and to follow may suffer a corrosive, invidious comparison.

Learning by imitation was first set forth systematically in Aristotle's writings on mimesis. The aim of imitation is *arete*, translatable as "excellence in action." The discipline of imitation is *paideia*. Neither the aim nor the execution is easy. The desire for excellence supposes recognition of one's own insufficiency: just muddling through is not the point. Clarity in execution is required, at least for Aristotle: the actions to be learned through imitation, the messages the mentor sends out, cannot be obscure or contradictory. Rules rule.

Another school of Greek thought, however, supposed that learning by example could occur through a more indirect process. Plato's Socrates was shy about laying down rules; he mostly asks questions. Part of the reason Socrates is indirect has to do with Plato's view of what it means really to understand something; knowledge has to take form with the knower himself, as something of his own possession—Plato's own version of craft knowledge. And part of Socrates' indirection derives from a challenge to his society.

For the Greeks of his time, imitation led inevitably to competition. You wanted to learn from others what to do only to do it better than they could; this was as true in the academies as in games or warfare. *Paideia* and *agon* were inseparable. Greek *agon* hid nothing; whether scholar, soldier, or athlete, the mentor knew you were out to best him, and the display of mastery over others was shame-free—an uninhibited bid for, as we would say, prestige. Plato's critique of this competitive display was that it foreclosed on the possibilities of exploration, of dwelling in difficulties. He took truly seriously the starting point of *arete*, the assumption of one's own insufficiency.

One strand of modern thinking frames the imitative/competitive impulse in quite the opposite way from Greek *agon*, though for much less worthy reasons than Plato's. It appears in Freud's view of the father as role model, who weighs so heavily, who so haunts his son—a burden the son seeks to cast off. The son competes by denying his father: "I didn't need you." The literary critic Harold Bloom has called this an anxiety of influence, as when the strongest influences on a poet are those the writer is most anxious to avoid acknowledging.

Perhaps just because our society celebrates *individual* initiative this urge appears; to deny or hide the influence of those whom one has emulated makes one's strengths and skills appear of one's own making. A role model's display of strength can indeed be suffocating to the person to whom it is directed. The doctor held his audience tight by asking, "If I could change myself, why can't you?" This question served as a shaming mirror, his accomplishments a negative reflection upon the sorry state of his listeners.

But there is another dimension which needs to be added to the relation between imitation and competition. Whether overt or covert, imitation invokes the dynamics of seduction. Not rape. The master wants to be embraced; the protégé embraces him by envy.

The Seductions of Inequality

The perverse, seductive power of inequality formed the subject of one of Rousseau's greatest essays, *Discourse on the Origin of Inequality* (as it was finally published in 1755), and the arguments he advances are of such contemporary importance that I want to present them in some detail.

Rousseau's starting point is this: invidious comparison could not hurt if we did not want to be someone different from the person we are. Different not just in material circumstances—a different person. Envy is a way of expressing that desire to become someone else. Modern society invites us to envy; in a world bent on destroying tradition and inherited place, on affirming the possibility of making something of ourselves through our own merits, what keeps us from becoming another person? All we have to do is imitate the sort of person we would like to be.

If we take up this invitation, however, we lose our self-respect. We are not innocent victims; no one is forcing us to be envious.

To explain how people participate in their own loss of self-respect, Rousseau draws a distinction between *amour de soi* and *amour-propre*. The French phrases separate, first of all, the ability to take care of oneself from the capacity to draw attention to oneself. In Rousseau's words:

> Amour propre and amour de soi . . . must not be confused. Amour de soi is a natural sentiment which inclines every animal to watch over its own preservation. . . . Amour propre is only a relative sentiment, artificial and born in Society, which inclines each individual to have a greater esteem for himself than for anyone else.[16]

So *amour de soi* is not "self-love"; it would better be expressed as "self-confidence," the conviction that we can maintain ourselves in the world. This confidence we acquire through the exercise of those solid craft labors which are our life support. And *amour-propre* is not merely a display of superiority, the demonstration of an inequality. Rousseau's biographer Maurice Cranston pithily defines *amour-propre* as "the desire to be superior to others *and* to be esteemed by them."[17] The second half requires their seduction; Rousseau focuses on their willingness to be seduced.

As *Discourse on the Origin of Inequality* unfolds, Rousseau works out how the self-respect of ordinary people fades through responding to the example set by others:

> He who sings or dances the best, he who is the most handsome, the strongest, and most adroit or the most eloquent becomes the most highly regarded; and this is the first step towards inequality, and at the same time towards vice.[18]

There seems nothing exceptional in this passage until we compare it to Nietzsche's in *Beyond Good and Evil:* "We have to force morals to bow down before hierarchy." Nietzsche's counsel is just to be strong, to take pride in yourself.[19] For Rousseau, the superior is not indifferent to the weak: their envy confirms he has something of value. How can he elicit it?

The superior is like a guard standing at a border crossing, simultaneously beckoning to others while refusing to accept their passports as valid. They insist; he then says, "Let me show you what a valid passport looks like." Now they are hooked: "But my passport looks just like that!" The seduction is about to occur: the guard ruefully demurs, "Well, it looks the same, but I'm not sure." And then is consummated; the immigrant looks at his documents and ruefully reflects, "My passport, although genuine, was not good enough."

I've put crudely the mechanics of invidious comparison which Rousseau descried in the Paris of his time, a city where elderly men dye their hair even though they know other people only notice the fact it is dyed; where solid bourgeois families ruin themselves to provide the carriages, houses, and clothes which, they also know, will yield them at most the ironic smiles of aristocrats willing occasionally to dine with them or condescend to borrow their money. More consequently for Rousseau, the same mechanics will lead the poor to abandon those pursuits which can sustain them—abandon them for chances in the street, for some magical encounter, some elevation of fortune which they keep a secret, knowing that those who know them well and wish them well would be appalled. Envy has the power to suspend one's judgment of reality. As a result, a person's *amour de soi*, be it graceful acceptance of age, station, or confidence in his or her own abilities, founders.

We may think that self-respect is the bedrock of character, but Rousseau did not. Desire for what one lacks seemed to him a much stronger force, and so *amour-propre* will always prevail over *amour de soi.*

The seductions of inequality seemed not only to Rousseau but to many of his contemporaries the dark side of the doctrine of careers open to talent.

In *The Wealth of Nations,* Smith wrote of the "overweening conceit which the greater part of men have of their abilities" and asserted, "The chance of gain is by every man more or less overvalued, and the chance of loss is by most men undervalued."[20] Competitive struggle in the marketplace would expose the cruel illusion of this "overweening conceit." Yet from envy the masses would persist, trying to emulate the risk-taking only the truly wealthy could afford. They would be seduced by possibility even though they had little chance of success.

The market economy also seemed to darken the word "open" in the call to arms "careers open to talent." The talented would form a self-righteous elect, invalidating the passports of the masses, a condition summoned to mind today by the phrase "the liberal elite." This is what worried, early on, the Scottish Enlightenment philosopher Adam Ferguson, who wrote in *An Essay on the History of Civil Society:*

> The separation of the professions, while it seems to promise improvement of skill . . . serves in some measure to break the bonds of society, to substitute mere forms and rules of art in place of ingenuity, and to withdraw individuals from the

common scene of occupation on which the sentiments of the
heart and the mind are most happily employed.[21]

Rousseau understood the other side of elitism: the fear of
being identified with the mass. The superior's *amour-propre*
depends on never being taken to be ordinary. While the liberal
elite may indeed identify with extremes of poverty or pain, the
ordinary person—the "loser," in American slang—arouses anxiety. That anxiety takes on a peculiar twist in the modern
emphasis on potential ability; this is an educational and labor
regime in which it becomes hard to develop something like
amour de soi, a realistic assessment and engagement of one's own
capacities. So fantasy, of the sort Smith also feared, is unleashed.

Against the seduction of envy, Rousseau argued for the
virtue of *amour de soi*, of craft, of the self-respect which consists
in doing something well for its own sake. His essay concludes
on a note of pessimism, however, just because he feared the
dynamics of seduction to be more powerful than those of self-
respect.[22] Other people have been taken too seriously, oneself
not enough.

These are some of the complications inequality raises in the
experience of respect, complications bred particularly by
unequal talents. As realistic egalitarians have been the first to
admit, nature distributes brains unequally, like beauty or art.
The question is what society makes of that fact. "Careers open
to talent" was a way to honor that inequality; it arose in an era
when talent could be framed and defined. Modern concepts of
potential ability take away the definition but not the inequality.

Talent itself, whether great or small, has an ambiguous relation to character, character which relates oneself to others. The crafting of self-respect can deny this connection, through inward obsession or object fixation. Displays of mastery can in principle provide a stronger connection, through furnishing models for guidance and imitation. In practice, however, imitation and competition have long been yoked together, the connection becoming an adversarial relation. And again, the display of mastery can trigger a dynamic of seduction in which the weak, when imitating the strong, only ratify inequality through envy.

Low Self-Esteem

The Enlightenment reformers who subscribed to the doctrine of natural aristocracy knew they had a problem, one summed up by the losing contestants at the cello contest: how to prevent people from becoming discouraged or resentful in the face of unequal talent. This is the problem of invidious comparison.

Beaumarchais's comedy of the time *The Marriage of Figaro* could also have been titled *Pepys's Revenge;* the play celebrated natural talent, Figaro triumphing over his dull-witted superiors. But the real problem of invidious comparison was better represented by Diderot's dialogue *Rameau's Nephew,* which was more the confession of one man who had fallen victim to the loss of *amour de soi* described by Rousseau; the fictional nephew of the great composer Rameau postures and denies his insignificance until, exhausted, he admits that he is little more than a shadow. As at the cello contest, invidious comparisons are drawn by the person likely to be wounded.

In the vocabulary of modern psychology, invidious comparisons of this sort lead to "low self-esteem." Modern social policies like personal mentoring or impersonal affirmative action seek to counter invidious comparisons which wound the self. It has been left to writers of a more political cast of mind to address the fundamental connection between inequality of talents and self-respect.

The thrust of these writers is that diversity should matter more than inequality—different kinds of ability should matter more than inequalities in any one talent. The legal philosopher Ronald Dworkin asserts, for instance, that because we "admire certain qualities of mind . . . the admiration should [not] take a material form"; society should not translate raw intelligence into privilege.[23] Like the psychologist Howard Gardner, he argues that intelligence is itself a bundle of quite various capacities; Gardner has shown that people possess visual intelligence as well as verbal skill, auditory as well as mathematical understanding, and such capacities are well-nigh impossible to represent by a single number, as in IQ tests. These writers focus on the variety of things individuals can do rather than how they compare.[24]

Moreover, there are good reasons to view societies in the same way. The economist Amartya Sen argued this case by analyzing the capacities of different societies to make use of the same resources; by a single monetary standard, for instance, China has been "smarter" in using equivalent amounts of foreign investment than India. But that single standard misleads, because China and India have different needs, and their particular "functionings," as Sen puts it, should be the basis of judging the uses to which they put their resources.[25]

These arguments which emphasize diversity rather than inequality are admirable, but they will not make the problem of low self-esteem go away. Though I may be proud to be Indian, the abler Chinese casts a shadow, and just because I feel overshadowed, I will not stop comparing myself to him. In a way that act is as old as humanity, the human propensity to envy and resent knowing no bounds of time and place. But in another way unequal ability established a certain historical trajectory for these sentiments.

The careers open to talent passed through a kind of social alchemy in the Enlightenment so that merit and talent became synonyms. The alchemy produced the modern term "meritocracy," coined by the British sociologist Michael Young in the same era Daniel Bell and Alain Touraine began writing about postindustrial society, the society based on skill. Meritocracy inhabits the same linguistic country as aptitude, fusing motivation, desire, and attitude with prowess and skill.

It's just the search to create an alchemical meritocracy which Nicholas Lemann abhorred among the devisers of aptitude tests whom he studied, particularly their effort to discover at ever earlier stages of the life cycle who "deserves" to be showered with society's largesse. In an impassioned conclusion to his study, he declared:

> Every society of course has positions of authority and expertise that must be filled by people who can execute them well. But the central, original principle of American meritocracy was different from this. It was that people should be chosen not for their suitability for specific roles but for their general worth, as if they were an updated Puritan elect.[26]

Michael Young, too, was a critic of his own word; he feared a new division between elite and mass, an able elite which feels it merits its privileges, a mass at once abashed and resentful of smart people. There's a deft moment in Young's satire, *The Rise of the Meritocracy, 1870–2033,* whose narrator is a brilliant graduate student in the twenty-first century: the young hotshot at the end claims that in the new meritocratic system "the lower classes no longer have the power to make revolt effective." A footnote at this point reveals that the author has been killed during an uprising by the low-IQ masses, meritocracy proving personally unbearable to them.[27]

Any researcher into social class is likely to come across one particular consequence of low self-esteem: its reverberation in the lives of those who ought to think with pride about their talents. In *Learning to Labor,* the British sociologist Paul Willis showed how young working-class adolescents held themselves back from progress in school for fear of standing out, "getting above themselves," losing ties to their friends if they went too far, losing touch with their communities. Personal ability is a double-edged weapon; using it may fulfill something in the individual's nature but at the cost of cutting ties to the world in which he or she has a place.[28] Those bonds, however, can diminish the sense that one has done what one should with oneself.

When I did the interviews in Boston for *The Hidden Injuries of Class,* the fear of young people to stick their heads above the parapet similarly appeared. But here, in families where the children in that pregnant meritocratic phrase "made something of themselves," the parents suffered from invidious comparison to their own children; they feared that their mobile offspring were becoming strangers to them, at worst that the children would become ashamed of them.

And in organizing mentoring sessions in Chicago, we had to figure out how to get around the fear of standing out among young people—and again the young doctor's example was no solution; he spoke in the name of hidden merit, but to uncover it the young blacks and Puerto Ricans would become strangers to their familiar selves. In all these practices of daily life, "meritocracy" stands for a threat to solidarity, felt by both potential winners and losers. Social mobility carries social costs.

One refinement made by proponents of diversity is that, in principle, different talents within a society should contribute to the common welfare. The original proponent of this view was, of course, Karl Marx; it is exemplified by his slogan "From each according to his ability, to each according to his need." In the practices of daily life, though, what good did it do his listeners that the young Puerto Rican was an eye doctor? Marx would answer that if he eventually returned to the community to practice, his ability would contribute to the common welfare. But this doesn't meet the issue: what illumination would his superiority provide his listeners in trying to understand themselves as part of the community?

Rather than a faulty solution to the problems of invidious comparison and low self-esteem, the proponents of diversity face a conundrum, which is simply that inequality is so basic a fact of human experience that people are constantly trying to make sense of it.

The best protection I'm able to imagine against the evils of invidious comparison is the experience of ability I've called craftwork, and the reason for this is simple. Comparisons, ratings, and testings are deflected from other people into the self; one sets the critical standard internally. Craftwork certainly does not banish invidious comparison to the work of others; it does refocus a person's energies, however, to getting an act right in itself, for oneself. The craftsman can sustain his or her self-respect in an unequal world.

In retrospect, I imagine our hostess in New York meant to convey something like this; merit lies ultimately in commitment to the notes. Otherwise, as the Leeds judge remarked, proving one's ability to others becomes a paralyzing effort.

Still, if the dignity of craft might provision self-respect, it does not dispose of the problem of mutual respect across the boundaries of inequality. Craftwork tends, indeed, to focus on the activity of making at the expense of interpersonal processes and relationships; it provides protection but also risks isolating the maker. The risks this isolation poses to the craftsman's own character become clearer in probing the second formulation of respect in modern society: respect accorded only to those who can, indeed, take care of themselves.

Chapter Four

The Shame of Dependence

Imagine a lover who declares, "Don't worry about me, I can take care of myself, I will never become a burden to you." We should show such a lover to the door; this nonneedy creature could never take our own needs seriously. In private life, dependence ties people together. A child who could not depend on adults for guidance would be a profoundly damaged human being, unable to learn, deeply insecure. As adults, if we avoided people sicker, older, weaker than ourselves who needed help, we would at best have a circle of acquaintances, not friends.

In the public realm, however, dependence appears shameful. It appears so particularly to modern welfare reformers. At a Labour Party conference recently the British prime minister declared that "the new welfare state must encourage work not dependency," in arguing for "compassion with a hard edge."[1] The hard human edge which eschews neediness and emphasizes self-sufficiency brings respect in the eyes of others and breeds self-respect.

Cabrini was just the sort of place welfare reformers thought to embody the evils of dependency. In my time, the late 1940s, it was a place for people who couldn't afford to house themselves. By the 1960s, it took care of broken families, teenage mothers, and drug addicts; the dependency was greater, the shame supposedly worse. It's impossible to know, fifty years on, if our white neighbors believed themselves demeaned; during Cabrini's later, grimmer days many inmates felt a surprising affection for "home." But certainly the outside world regarded their condition as demeaning; something had to be done to save them from themselves. In Cabrini, the welfare reformers resorted in the end to the ultimate solution: recently much of the project has been destroyed, the houses bulldozed, the land leveled; on it are now rising expensive, quite beautiful townhouses.

The impulse to wean people from dependency now moves welfare reform in a much wider sphere, in unemployment benefits, medical care, schooling, and old-age provision. The old welfare state policed the needy, but the reformers want to set the needy free of the state: no long-term life on the dole, medical insurance people pay for, schooling they choose, pensions they manage for themselves. This widening compass of reform only deepens the puzzling divide between the private and the public sides of dependence. The need of others so compelling in love, friendship, and parenting is pressed inward by the conviction that dependency is shameful.

The "Infantilization Thesis"

The belief that dependence demeans derives in the liberal canon from a concept of adulthood. This view was well expressed by the leading twentieth-century American welfare reformer, Senator Daniel Patrick Moynihan, early in his career. "To be poor is an objective condition; to be dependent, a subjective one as well," he then believed. "Being poor is often associated with considerable personal qualities; being dependent rarely so." The explanation he arrived at for the subjective corruption of the pauper, of the welfare client, was that "[dependency] is an incomplete state in life: normal in the child, abnormal in the adult."[2]

He applied to the welfare state a long-standing argument in political thought which could be called the "infantilization thesis." Liberal thinkers have supposed that dependency, particularly dependency on government, makes adults behave like children. Kant dramatically and succinctly put forward the infantilization thesis which today animates American and British welfare reformers:

> Enlightenment is Man's emergence from his self-incurred immaturity. *Immaturity* is the inability to use one's own understanding without the guidance of another. This immaturity is *self-incurred* if its cause is not lack of understanding, but lack of resolution and courage to use it without the guidance of another. The motto of enlightenment is therefore: *Sapere aude!* Have the courage to use your *own* understanding![3]

This is to make childhood and adulthood, immaturity and maturity, into political categories; the phenomenon of dependency divides them.

A century before Kant, John Locke explored why an adult might behave in public like a needy child in one of liberalism's founding texts, the *Two Treatises of Government* of 1690. Locke's nemesis was the statesman Sir Robert Filmer, who maintained that the absolute power of kings resembles the authority of a father over his children.[4] Locke accepted the reign of a father over his children as one of just dominion and submission. But that power is legitimate, in his view, only because the capacity to reason independently is undeveloped in the child. As adults grow, they become more able to judge and act rationally, and so to govern themselves; they thus can move from private to public life.

> His command over his children is but temporary . . . a discipline to their education . . . yet his power extends not to their liberty when they are once arrived to . . . the years of discretion. The father's empire then ceases, and he can from thencefoward no more dispose of the liberty of his son than that of any other man.[5]

A legitimate state should enable the young to free themselves from this yoke.

What happens if the state blocks the capacity to reason independently and rationally as an adult? Then, in psychological lingo, adults regress to childhood as it was experienced in the private realm. In advancing this idea, Locke spoke not only as Filmer's antagonist, but as a sociological observer of courts— notoriously the English court of Charles II, though his observations would apply with even greater force slightly later to the French court of Louis XIV at Versailles, both filled with dukes and duchesses devoted to playtime. The court's fripperies, deep intrigues for the most trivial favors, mindless boredom, and endless search for amusement came at the expense of rational self-sovereignty; these were truly "children of the king." They had no being but his command, no desire but his wish.

The sharp-eyed reader will notice that Kant and Locke do not quite agree. For the former, adult immaturity is "self-incurred," for the latter social and political conditions force men to behave like boys—a disagreement becoming of great importance to later welfare policy. But the philosophers concurred in conceiving the remedy for the dishonor of dependence. This consists in exercising rational self-sovereignty in one's acts as much as possible; in particular, in taking nothing the powerful say as true simply because one depends on them. Judging rationally for oneself makes one an adult.

And so one earns the regard of others: the "infantilization thesis" profoundly shaped modern beliefs about mutual respect. The courtier is contemptible because a parasite; the citizen is honorable because self-maintaining. But classic liberal codes of public honor did not quite use the word "self" as it is meant today; the liberal fathers did not speak of individualism. That word "individualism" belongs to a later time, Alexis de Tocqueville coining it in the 1830s to describe the social isolation he witnessed in America. It since has come to imply a denial of social connection—a denial which reached an apotheosis in the famous declaration of the British prime minister Margaret Thatcher that "there is no society, only individuals and their families."[6]

Classic liberalism never subscribed to such a view. Nor did it suppose the rational self to be well-balanced in desire or well-coordinated in action. Mill writes somewhere of experience as a relentless ringing of alarm bells. The need to prevent experience from falling into unrelated bits and pieces can be met only through the exercise of one's own reason, rather than reliance upon others to do the management, no matter how rational their plans. The liberal conception of maturity has indeed a "hard edge"; it emphasizes the sheer struggle for self-control.[7]

Denial of the opportunity to act like an adult is the great Lockean fear. Translated into the early conditions of Cabrini, Locke's fear would have been aroused by the fact that the authorities hesitated not for a moment to intervene the way they did, once the glass wars came to light. The residents were meant to receive help, rather than deal with the problem themselves; they were demeaned because they were treated like children.

In the wider realm of the welfare state, this liberal conviction carries an undeniable justice. The patient to whom a doctor explains nothing, the student taught by rote commands, the employee who is ignored—all have become spectators to their own needs, objects worked upon by a superior power. Communist practice could be found as well on this side of dependency's coin; spectatorship dominated everyday life beneath the crusts of collective ideology.

It should be said that social thinkers and writers who cannot be labeled liberals have equally feared passive dependency of a willing sort. That dishonorable condition appeared in the seventeenth-century philosopher Etienne de La Boétie's evocation of "voluntary servitude":

. . . so many men, so many villages, so many cities, so many nations, sometimes suffer under a single tyrant who has no other power than the power they give him; who could do them absolutely no injury unless they preferred to put up with him rather than contradict him . . . it is therefore the inhabitants themselves who permit, or rather, bring about, their own servitude.[8]

"Man is born a rebel," Dostoevsky's Grand Inquisitor declares, a rebelliousness which carries the curse of conflicting desires. Only a demeaning, willing passivity, only blind obedience, will relieve the curse:

> Man seeks to worship what is incontestable, so incontestable, indeed, that all men at once agree to worship it all together. For the chief concern of these miserable creatures is not only to find something that I or someone else can worship, but to find something that all believe in and worship, and the absolutely essential thing is that they should do so *all together*.[9]

Of all those who have invoked the shame of dependency, it could justly be said that they have a horror of the primal maternal scene: the infant sucking at the mother's breast. They fear that through force or desire, adult men will continue to suckle; the mother's breast becomes the state. What's distinctive about liberalism is its view of the man who disengages his lips; he becomes a citizen.

Dependence and the Work Ethic

When the founders of the American Republic equated the upright citizen with the man who works, they had a particular kind of worker in mind, the sturdy yeoman tilling his own soil or the independent craftsman.[10] It is easy to understand why these kinds of workers fit into the liberal tradition; these workers largely controlled their own labors. Industrial labor and technology was just beginning at the end of the eighteenth century, appearing for instance in cloth-weaving, the production of glass, and some construction products like nails.

It may seem an irony that as industrial capitalism progressed, the worker having ever less control over his or her work, still this liberal tradition lived on. But now it served as a rebuke to capitalists rather than to kings. The independent craftsman, taking pride in his work, dependent only on his skill, served as a rebuke to a system which treated industrial workers like beasts of burden. The dignity of craft could be made a sentimental subject, as in the writings and projects of John Ruskin, who invented a medieval past filled with fulfilled artisans to contrast to the degradation of workers in the industrial system. But this same liberal ideal could take a more practical and sharp-edged turn, as in the efforts of William Morris to reorganize industrial technologies and practices to make workers more in control of their work. The wallpapers Morris designed are as innovative in their production as beautiful in their look, mass-produced but not by drones; the workers in Morris's workshops controlled the speed of their work, made judgments about the quality of papers and pigments.

The work ethic invoked by Max Weber is removed in one way from the collision between liberal values and industrial capitalism: Weber himself seemed not much interested in experiments with industrial technology, which he simply swept into the larger and more abstract category of "rationalization" of labor. The Protestant work ethic itself is a kind of perversion of liberal values; the work ethic drove people to prove their worth, to show they were independent, purposeful, determined, but show it through denying themselves pleasures—yet no proof ever felt good enough. The driven man strove constantly to furnish new evidences of his worth.

What drew capitalists and industrial laborers together in the first age of industrial capitalism, and socialists like Morris together with more rigid manufacturers, was belief in work itself as the single most important source of both mutual respect and self-respect. Sloth is of course a sin recorded in the most ancient biblical texts; most poor people had no choice but to avoid it if they wanted to eat. But as the historian Johann Huizinga reminds us, the absolute moral value put on work, the supremacy of work over leisure, the fear of wasting time, of being unproductive—this is a value which only takes hold of all of society, the rich as well as the poor, in the nineteenth century.[11] Liberalism's respected adult worked.

This value made its way into the nascent welfare state. From the early nineteenth century on, social reformers had distinguished between paupers who lived on poor relief and the working poor who did not. Paupers were thought "not simply poor but degraded, their character corrupted and their will sapped through reliance on charity," observe Nancy Fraser and Linda Gordon.[12] Here was Kant's view applied to welfare: a "self-incurred" loss of integrity would occur through the refusal to work, and so the point of welfare policy, particularly in Britain, was to strengthen the characters of the poor by forcing them to work, no matter what work they did.

The contrast between worker and pauper has had an affirmative side of sorts. In asserting that "to be poor is an objective condition" and that "being poor is often associated with considerable personal qualities," Senator Moynihan, like nineteenth-century reformers, aimed to draw the sting of contempt from sheer poverty, affirming the dignity of the poor who worked at even the most menial jobs.

The pauper may suffer, in modern welfare jargon, from low self-esteem, because of depression or the fear of being tested. Still, the moralization of work meant that the unproductive elicited little pity. When the person on charity says, "I cannot," his provider may think, "You don't want to." From this came the particularly punitive character of workhouses in Britain, and also in America, so shocking to Mediterranean or Russian visitors.

In a famous book on the history of childhood, *Centuries of Childhood,* Philippe Ariès sought to show how the period human beings spend in the dependent conditions of childhood has stretched out in the course of modern history. In Locke's time, he observes, a human being aged eight or nine was treated as an "incipient adult," accorded adult powers and responsibilities, marrying even before he or she could biologically procreate. Whereas modern childhood extends beyond puberty; a new category—adolescence—has been invented to fill out the years before which adulthood begins.[13]

In part, so elemental a fact as advances in medicine can explain this change; in Locke's time men and women in their fifties were considered old, and today the twenty years of childhood and adolescence still constitute only a quarter of a healthy life span. But the change can also be accounted, culturally, by the new emphasis on work. To work well requires an ever longer period of training and discipline. Very few of the arguments for universal education or against child labor in the nineteenth century invoke the idea of protecting the child from the work world; rather, they speak of preparing him or her for it.

Education itself becomes increasingly oriented to that task; the classical education provided by places like Oxford and Cambridge fall under increasing attack as elitist, while learning oriented to working justifies the spread of mass education. By a peculiar play of reflections in the mirror of class, the young man lounging in his Oxford college comes a moral pauper, living off the labors of others, doing nothing productive, learning nothing useful.

The dislike of paupers, the equation of an unproductive life with a defective character, held sway over nineteenth-century revolutionaries and radicals as much as over bourgeois charity workers or educational reformers. Marx's contempt for the lumpen proletariat derived directly from his enemies' view of paupers—the character of the lumpen proletariat corrupted by servility and blind need. To Marx, these wretched souls asserted themselves only in fits of disorganized, mindless violence; effective militant action required a self-control the lumpen proletariat lacked; the revolutionary is closer in spirit to Weber's driven man. Outside the often puritanical confines of Marx's writings, other socialists focused on the lack of work, the insufficiency of charity as a way of life, because the lack of work demeans something in a person's soul.

There is a caveat to be made about equating work with worth, a caveat which appears concretely in Cabrini. At the project's beginnings, during and just after the Second World War, most able-bodied men worked, both black and white. Did the marriage between work and the liberal fear of dependence not apply to them?

Private home ownership is a compelling desire in American society. Perhaps the origins of this desire can be traced back to the homesteading impulse. If there's any substance to the history of American individualism, a large amount consists in the urge to own where you live. In the nineteenth century, the aim of much working-class effort was to save enough at work to buy a home, and only scrimping off wages would make this possible. Few banks then lent mortgage money to American workers, the government almost never. By the time Cabrini was built, quite a few working-class Americans had achieved this symbol of independence; banks and government had loosened up somewhat and about 60 percent of the Chicago working class owned, through mortgages or free and clear, their own homes. But the people in Cabrini didn't have this resource, and market rents were out of their reach.

Traditionally it has fallen to men to provide shelter, a part of the male portfolio of competence. But in the Cabrini generation succeeding mine, that role was shouldered by single-parent women. Analysts debate whether the welfare system itself broke up many black marriages, or whether the family systems of these poor people took, since slavery, a different course from that of the nuclear family. For whatever reason, by the 1960s many women were facing the responsibility of providing shelter and were not able to meet it alone.

Here's how the dishonor of dependence, defined in terms of needing public housing, felt to one such mother:

I'm not depending on what somebody else is going to offer me. . . . But I know I have four kids, so if they do offer me something, it will be worth it. . . . I mean, I'm trying to make

it just like the next person. I'm not asking them for no hand-
outs either, but why would you deny me an opportunity when
you're talking about that you want to [have] people in them
that really want to maintain them?[14]

It's a confusing statement because she is confused about her role
in taking help to make a home for her four children. More
largely, issues of race and gender have meant that public housing in America has carried more stigma than social housing in
Britain or Northern Europe. Work isn't what's bothering her;
dependence is.

This caveat, however, indicates the very sweep of the liberal
formulation: rather than hinge simply on labor, it more inclu-
sively lays its emphasis on adulthood. The issue is adult self-
sovereignty.

What then is wrong with this liberal version of respect? The
liberal horror of adult dependency has served to challenge power
which demands servility, which renders citizens spectators to
their own needs. The liberal fathers meant to establish the dignity of citizens, as adults. And yet they were poor psychologists.

Dependence Separated from Shame

Modern psychology understands maturation very differently
from the views of political liberalism. The liberal fathers drew
a sharp contrast between childhood and adulthood to show the
passage from private to public definitions of dependency. That
sharp contrast supposed that human maturation into the adult
public realm is akin to a moth emerging from a chrysalis. This
view is enacted into law when an age of consent is established

for sexual relations, or an age at which the reasoning adult is suddenly entitled to vote.

What modern psychologists, Freudian or otherwise, dispute about the chrysalis image is the suggestion of a transformative moment at which the past is—or should be—entirely left behind. Most developmental psychologists assume there is a constant passage back and forth between childhood and adult experience. This is the work memory does; rather than simply recovering facts about the past, memory goes back and forth between past and present, reworking and reinterpreting. "Regression" to an immature state means recovering the ages you have lived through, rather than being a child again; the adult consciously connected to the child he or she has once been has a deeper understanding of the present.[15] For this reason, regression to childhood has a far richer and more positive meaning to Freud than it did to Locke; regression forms part of the psychodynamic of reasoning.

Of course, liberal politicians are not elected for their views on regression. They may want genuinely to rescue people from a degrading dependency, as well as to save the government money. But the coupling of shame and dependency is culture-specific, and it's useful to keep in mind just how culturally specific.

The Japanese word *amae*, for instance, represents quite a different kind of adult and public dependency. In Japanese culture, people surrender to other adults, expecting to be cared for as by right. Businessmen and politicians do so, as well as paupers. Among strangers in cities, for instance, *amae* becomes the practice of *tanomu*; *tanomu* behavior seems to dramatize the sheer fact of helplessness—weak deferential smiles, hands turned out slightly in appeal. Strangers in the Japanese cities who practice *tanomu* in asking for directions, in shopping, or in bars expect, however, to reciprocate themselves. Each moment of surrender creates an immediate connection to people who don't know one other.[16] The psychiatrist Takeo Doi uneasily likens *amae* to what Western psychoanalysis calls "passive object-love."[17] Uneasily, because in Japan surrender is not a loss of face; shame comes to the person who fails to respond, shame comes to the indifferent individual.

So, if no surprise, the liberal conviction proves no universal truth. But in our own culture, psychologists have unhitched dependency and shame by making another distinction, that between shame and guilt. A criminal who successfully robs a bank may later feel guilty about what he has done; a robber who bungles the job may feel shame. Or, to use measures of ability rather than bank robbery, you feel guilty if you cheat on a test, shame if you fail. The difference lies between transgression, which produces guilt, and inadequacy, which produces shame.

Guilt is in Freud's view two-sided: since every person has the capacity to hurt others, especially those whom one loves, that very knowledge might prod one's conscience so that one fears to transgress against them. Freud's contemporary Alfred Adler formulated shame as, in his celebrated term, an "inferiority complex." A loyal socialist if eventually a disloyal Freudian, Adler believed that competitive experiences in the market economy were most likely to breed shame in adult workers; market failure is the source for this loss of self-esteem. Psychoanalysis after Freud did not follow in Adler's path. Adler supposed shame comes from without, in the workings of capitalism; Freud's heirs supposed shame was generated within.

This view, embodied in different ways by Gerhart Piers and Sylvan Tompkins, can be traced back to an observation by Hegel about sex. Hegel speaks of "love that is not complete" and says that "there is still something inimical in oneself which keeps love from reaching completion and perfection."[18] Modern psychology has expanded this observation to other forms of experience which feel as though they fall short of completion and consummation. Gerhart Piers, for instance, emphasizes shame as an inner sense of incompleteness, whatever the hard evidence of achievement or gratification; the person who fails to achieve "fulfillment" imagines there is something wrong with himself or herself.[19] Just that feeling of inadequacy can never be separated from imagining an ideal Other: someone else, somewhere, is achieving fulfillment.[20]

In Adler's version or in Piers's, shame has to do with competition rather than dependence. The inferiority complex implies a deep consciousness of other people, to be sure, but it is the kind of consciousness evoked by Rousseau's territory, one in which envy is at work. The inferiority complex, whether generated from without or within, objectively or subjectively, means making an invidious comparison in such a way that whoever one is and whatever one has seem not good enough.

This looks nothing like the emotions aroused by dependence on a doctor, on a colonel, on a social worker—not to speak of dependence on a parent, lover, or friend. Just needing them does not produce shame.

The inferiority complex poses a question about modern efforts at welfare reform. Welfare reformers have imagined that in forcing people to work, a demeaning chapter would close in their lives. But another chapter may then open. If Adler is right, just the fact that these new workers are likely to be at the bottom of the occupation heap will breed a sense of inferiority; if Piers is right, they will enter into the more "normal" condition of internal, impossible longing for what they lack. Either way, inequality eats into respect; invidious comparison takes the place of sheer neediness, and true shame begins.

Psychological investigation puts forward a second and equally important aspect of shame which divorces this sentiment from the experience of dependence. This refers to "loss of face," or to the "nakedness of shame," metaphors which convey a particular subjective experience. Again Freud is the starting point but not the end of the story. In *Three Essays on the Theory of Sexuality* he ties shame explicitly to the naked body; he does so because of the German word itself for shame, *Scham*. In both men and women, *die Scham* names the genital zone; the pubic mound is *Schamberg*, pubic hair *Schamhaare*.[21] In *Three Essays* Freud therefore took shameful exposure to be an erotic exhibition.

After Freud, the sexual component has mattered less, the social conditions of exposure more. Thus the psychoanalyst Erik Erikson, in an elegantly simple formula, proposes that shame occurs when someone is rendered "visible and yet [is] not ready to be visible," apparent, for instance, when a child struggling to read is being singled out by a teacher for making a mistake.[22] Sylvan Tompkins finds something cunning about the experience of exposure; he instances the "child who covers his face in the presence of the stranger, but who also peeks through his fingers so that he may look without being seen."[23]

The "nakedness of shame" thus refers to losing control over what is being revealed. The adult analogue would be to the white parents in Cabrini after the nearly fatal glass war; the behavior of their children was publicly laid bare by invading social workers before the parents were ready to expose it to view.

It would be a psychological error to equate the fear of exposure with privacy, just because the private realm is one in which people feel free to open up, and in particular to expose their weaknesses and needs. As Niklas Luhmann has observed, the intimate sphere defines a degree of trust between individuals which would be misplaced in their relation to institutions.[24] Nor is fear of exposure a matter of hiding a guilty secret. My point is that the statement "I need help" falls into a different category; there's nothing inherently shameful about it, so long as it can be *managed* by the person who makes it.

In the private realm, just as few parents are ashamed of their children per se when the children misbehave, so the wise parent does not hide his or her child's misdeeds from others—such secrecy ultimately will harm the child. What adults, like children, need is to control the conditions under which they see and are seen.

Lockean liberalism put a great emphasis on the transparency of political relationships, fearing secret state powers hidden away from the scrutiny of citizens. Locke's ideas are an important source, for instance, for modern demands for freedom of information. But his legacy had a more paradoxical aspect, in the desire to make social relations as transparent as political ones. Wanting to know who people "really" are risks shaming them. It gives them no room to hide.

One of the cultural consequences of this tradition is to make people feel demeaned if they have to ask for help, or expose their weaknesses. I sometimes imagined in later mentoring sessions in Chicago that my charges were avid readers of Locke, so difficult was it to get them to admit, "I don't know that word," or "I don't know what a square root is," as though the admission of weakness were indeed demeaning; trust in the mentor begins at the moment when the protégé freely asks for help.

Again this fear to expose one's weakness is culture-specific. In the Indian villages studied by Louis Dumont, people constantly appeal to each other for help if they are too old, too sick, or too muddled to do something for themselves; Dumont says that he began to address his own Western prejudices once he stopped writing up his reports on this behavior using the word "shameless." As a Westerner, he at first meant it as a pejorative, but for them, appeals for help were literally without shame.[25]

In the course of studying people at work, the fear of asking for help more and more impressed me as a reliable sign of a dysfunctional organization. Asking for help too often sends out a signal that the worker is "needy"—but how often is too often? At one high-tech firm I studied, the usual answer was not to ask for help until something went wrong. The employees feared appearing needy for good reason; their employers understandably didn't like being asked to sort out messes, and they wanted employees they didn't have to "mother." But the fear of asking for help and so appearing needy meant that information flows in the organization dried up; problems became evident only after they had become, indeed, messes.

We might in this regard want to reconsider the invocation to the sturdy yeoman, the independent craftsman, or today the consultant, as the Jeffersonian ideal of an adult citizen. Celebration of this ideal may be disempowering to others whose need for help they are ashamed to voice—producing in the polity, as in the high-tech company, a discussion of needs only after things have become a mess.

Autonomy

To avoid the problems evoked by the sturdy yeoman while preserving a sense of personal distinctiveness, psychology uses the term "autonomy" and contrasts it to independence. "Autonomy" has, however, proved a divisive word in psychoanalysis.

One school, exemplified by Erik Erikson, conceives of autonomy as a process in converting necessity into desire; a child must deal with the problem of "wanting to do what he is supposed to do," as in control of feces.[26] The reward for converting necessity into desire is self-respect; in Erikson's words, the child learns "self-control without loss of self-esteem."[27]

Psychologists like D. W. Winnicott interpreted autonomy as the capacity to treat other people as different from oneself; understanding that separation gives both others and oneself autonomy. To Winnicott, experiencing the autonomy of another person can be as basic as an infant running her fingers over a mother's skin, sensing it is different. Like his contemporary John Bowlby, Winnicott believed that this perception of difference plays a positive role in forging a social bond. For instance, the young child learns what the mother can do which the child cannot do for himself; as the child matures, the lives of people whom the child trusts become ever more sharply etched unlike his own. We commonly think of "autonomy" as the capacity to separate from others, which is a self-referential use of the word. Winnicott describes autonomy as a strength of character based on perceptions of others; that is, it establishes a relationship between people, rather than an isolating difference—the child developing autonomy can see and engage outside himself or herself.[28]

The views of Bowlby and Winnicott illumine a crucial element in treating others with respect: what might be called the grant of autonomy to others. Yet this grant of autonomy is not fixed or irrevocable like a grant of property. Autonomy is constantly being renewed in subjective life, lost and gained, as social conditions change.

The interviewer's "error" in identifying with his or her subjects, which I described in my own professional practice, helps explain why. An initial emotional connection occurs between adults in confusing self and other. This confusion is what Adam Smith calls "sympathy." In *The Theory of Moral Sentiments* (1759–61), he declares that sympathy for the plight of another arises when a person "endeavor[s] . . . to put himself in the situation of the other, and to bring home to himself every little circumstance of distress which can possibly occur to the sufferer . . . in its minutest incidents."[29]

Sympathy is no generalizing sentiment; it requires feeling in those "minutest incidents" that you and I have had the same experience. Autonomy builds on this connection, but changes its character. Your experience becomes like the child touching a mother's skin; gradually I perceive how different the details of your experience are from mine, but I do not withdraw my mental hand. The self-criticism an interviewer has to make about errors of identification also attends other relations; in sensing how you differ from me, I know more about who I am as a distinctive person.

It's just this rhythm of identification and differentiation that characterizes the process of autonomy, among adults as among children, a process that has constantly to be renewed. There is a further and crucial consequence: I accept that I may not understand you. A family would break apart if this grant did not occur: all communication would be homogenized, what parents or children learned from their incommensurate experience would be excluded. Similarly in education or medicine: we grant autonomy to teachers or doctors when we accept that they know what they are doing, even if we don't understand it; the same autonomy ought to be granted the pupil or the patient, because they know things about learning or being sick which the person teaching or treating them might not fathom.

Conceived in this way, autonomy is a powerful recipe for equality. Rather than an equality of understanding, a transparent equality, autonomy means accepting in the other what you do not understand, an opaque equality. In so doing, you are treating the fact of their autonomy as equal to your own. But to avoid the virtuoso's mastery, the grant must be mutual.

Rather surprisingly, Locke accepts this. The people have to rationally understand and consent to the laws they obey; in that sense Locke wants power to be entirely transparent. But once consent is given, matters change. Locke's synonym for autonomy is "prerogative," and in the *Second Treatise* he writes that "prerogative is nothing but the power of doing public good without a rule."[30] Shouldn't the good ruler follow the explicit dictates of laws? Locke is not quite convinced. The people have to believe in and trust their ruler; when they trust, they grant him a measure of freedom to act without constant auditing, monitoring, and oversight. Lacking that autonomy, he could indeed never make a move.

The intellectual drama of liberalism lies partly in the way this acceptance of autonomy conflicts with belief in rational judgment. Sympathy fits into rational, transparent acts of consent; the citizen and ruler should be able to identify with the experience of the other. Lack of mutual understanding invites abuse of power. Yet without the citizen's granting of autonomy to the ruler, the state, like the family, will break down.

What does granting autonomy to others do to the sense of self? Some psychologists are prone to give an optimistic answer to this question: acknowledging others strengthens the self. A person or group lacking self-confidence is unlikely to express admiration for the achievements of others; anxieties about self-worth are going to make people withhold rather than grant respect—the dynamics of the zero-sum game come into play. In Winnicott's clinical practice, he thus sought to break down that game by focusing patients on the genuine worth of others; in so doing, they might come to think more easily about their own value.

Just here, liberal thinkers about adult independence could reasonably object. In society, a poor man's self-confidence is hardly going to be strengthened by expressing admiration for the wealth of the capitalist or the superior education of the nuclear scientist. Another reasonable objection concerns craftwork; of course one learns by imitating a master whom one admires, but true self-confidence is achieved when one no longer needs that model and can do good work for oneself; now the homage matters less.

The quarrel here between psychology and politics turns on a question of process. The psychologists believe in an essential passing back and forth between people, a constant give and take, which produces the experience of distinction, the awareness of difference, the granting of autonomy—subjective awareness which lasts only so long as the process of personal interaction continues. The liberal political thinkers instead believe that while independence and autonomy are outcomes of human interactions, these results outlast the processes which produced them. Just as one can't undo becoming an adult, so one can't undo the consequences of education or the accumulation of wealth. At a certain point, the craftsman stops asking for direction. Liberalism has argued that freedom is also something which transcends give and take. Its rational forms and formulations become fixed in laws.

There's justice on both sides of this argument. For people in societies where liberty is lacking, everyday interpersonal processes may not generate much hope for change. But the opposite error is to assume that even in the most repressive societies people learn nothing at all from daily relationships, minute fluctuations, and mutual adjustments. This is especially true of the experience of mutual respect, and especially in repressive regimes; lacking a grand formula, a rational exposition, small acts may signal a recognition of the worth of another—acts so small they cannot be seen, and so repressed, by the state.

The nineteenth-century sociologist Emile Durkheim believed, in the words of one of his interpreters, that "social cohesion occurs because one person is always dependent upon another to achieve a feeling of completeness."[31] Dependency supposes incompleteness in oneself; completeness requires the resources of another which one may well not understand.

Durkheim's own solution to respect for inequalities of talent was to argue that in the complex web of social interactions, things will even out, and everyone has something special to contribute: dependency will resolve itself into interdependency. Under these conditions the grant of autonomy, in which respect for the other dwells, can be freely given.

In Cabrini, I can easily see how a tough-minded thinker of Locke's sort might think these formulas just so much social-worker talk, covering up the basic fact that people were in the grip of the Nanny State; the managers of the housing project did not make any practical grant of autonomy to their charges. And yet something of the vigor of liberal advocacy was weakened by its own often naive and one-dimensional assumptions about human character. This tradition could never make sense of how the lessons of character learned in private might be carried over into the public realm, making politics *richer* for carrying real psychological weight.

Particularly has this been true of the liberal imagination of dependence. Dependency has appeared like a coin with two faces, one private, the other public; on one side the need of others appears dignified, on the other side shaming. The dignity of dependence never appeared to liberalism a worthy political project.

The last time I visited the project was a few years ago, to attend a ceremony marking the beginning of its destruction. It was a glorious, cool, clear day in the city; bulldozers, cleaned and shined, were parked at the ready. A housing commissioner spoke, invoking the need to renew the community once again and promising the surviving tenants a better place to live elsewhere in the city; they would not be able to afford to live here anymore. It was as though the fifty years of lack could be abolished the moment the bulldozers were turned on, as though this blighted memory would be erased from the city's consciousness. As I watched the first bulldozer pile into the house where my mother and I had lived, it seemed to me I was witnessing a truly shameful "solution" to dependence.

Chapter Five

Compassion
Which Wounds

The Nun and the Socialist

Jane Addams, Chicago's most notable social worker, was a heroine to my mother's generation. She helped make social work into a professional career for women; active in international socialist movements, Addams won the Nobel Peace Prize in 1931. She did battle with a near-saint after whom Cabrini Green was named. Frances Xavier Cabrini was an Italian nun who migrated to the United States in 1889, becoming the champion of poor immigrants to America. Addams made a politics out of reserve, out of learning to keep silent about her own compassion. To Mother Cabrini, that silence was anathema.

"Poor visiting" in the nineteenth century was often a hobby for middle-class women, at worst a swooping down on the homes of poor women in order to offer advice on child-rearing, clothes-making, or cooking (usually performed in the bourgeois home by servants, not the visitors themselves). The histo-

rian of Victorian charity Gertrude Himmelfarb divides compassion into sentimental and nonsentimental forms, the first
aimed at feeling good, the second at doing good.[1] Visiting the
poor was sentimental compassion. To put social work on a professional footing, Addams believed, middle-class women had to
break the mind-set of sentimental charity.

Mother Cabrini also sought to reform poor visiting. But for
her, the social worker served the poor only in order to serve
God; on the eve of her departure for America, Mother Cabrini
declared, "My God . . . if I could only extend my arms to
embrace the world as a gift to you."[2] This might seem ultimately sentimental, hardly a professional attitude. In Chicago
before the First World War, however, Mother Cabrini's version
of social work proved practical. She spoke quite openly about
what her immigrant charges lacked: their poor English, their
absent education, their primitive ideas of hygiene. She provided
them teachers, doctors—and money. She provided for them;
she almost ostentatiously did good.

Suspicion about being good—Himmelfarb's "sentimental
compassion"—has a long pedigree in the annals of charity. The
benefactor aroused suspicions for a reason Nathaniel Hawthorne
put succinctly: "Benevolence is the twin of pride."[3] The motto
of an influential nineteenth-century British organization, the
Charity Organization Society, was "Not Alms, but a Friend";
the meaning of that motto was explained by one member of the
C.O.S. as follows:

> The chief need of the poor today [is] not alms-giving, but the
> moral support of true friendship—the possession of a real
> friend, whose education, experience, and influence, whose
> general knowledge of life, or special knowledge of domestic

economy are placed at the service of those who have neither the intelligence, the tact nor the opportunity to extract the maximum of good from their slender resources.[4]

A comparison is made here to the credit of the "true friend" who helps his or her more limited brethren. The comparison makes the "slender resources" of those helped into a kind of stage backdrop from which the true friend steps forward toward the footlights.

Addams knew she had, first of all, to remove acts of compassion from becoming morally self-serving. In Chicago, she created Hull House, a "settlement house." The settlement house was a British invention, a community center where workers could further their education, eat, and deal with local problems. The most famous, Toynbee Hall in Whitechapel, founded by Samuel Barnett in 1884, served the Whitechapel community in the East End of London; Jane Addams visited it annually from 1887 to 1889. Both in America and Europe the settlement houses allied themselves to mutual aid societies, which operated as a kind of self-directing welfare system for the poor. These societies provided insurance, and in some cases mortgage money for housing.[5]

The role of the social workers in these efforts was that of practical adviser. Under no circumstances was the will of the social worker to prevail over the democratic decisions of the residents. Addams had dramatic evidence in Chicago of the anger which an authoritarian, benevolent regime could arouse. This was the Pullman Strike of 1894.

Pullman was a railway magnate who in the 1880s founded a town for workers in which he provided housing, schools, and parks. Pullman, Illinois, differed sharply from the workers' community financed by Robert Owen in New Lanark; Pullman himself owned everything. Pullman, Illinois, differed from the phalansteries which Fourier imagined for Paris; work itself was not redesigned, rather the community surrounding work. But something drove Pullman to his own cost; his benefactions nearly ruined him.

The workers in his model town rose up against him and his kindly despotism during a strike in 1894, one of the most violent in American labor history. In an article written for *Survey Magazine* in 1912, Addams tried to explain their anger by comparing the capitalist to Shakespeare's patriarch King Lear. Of Lear's relation to the rebellious Cordelia, Addams remarked, "It was impossible for him to calmly watch his child developing beyond the strength of his own mind . . . it was new to him that his child should be moved by a principle outside himself. . . ." Of Pullman's relation to his workers, she observed that the industrialist wanted to own how they thought.[6]

A membrane so porous between caring and controlling that it dissolves at the slightest touch: Addams's perception of this dilemma made her no less ambivalent about socialist than about capitalist benefactors. In 1900, Addams had attended the great exposition in Paris, "haunting the fair's working-class housing displays, hoping they might show a way out of the violent passions that had engulfed . . . all of Chicago in 1894."[7] The socialist schemes seemed to her, however, just to embody more of the Lear problem, glorifying the political virtue of the sponsors. Similarly, she doubted Beatrice Webb, the British Fabian socialist; Webb, imperially self-confident, seemed to cross the line between being of service and being seen to be of service. To Addams this presaged that Webb would ultimately be rejected by the masses in whose name she spoke, just as George Pullman had been.

For these reasons, in the settlement houses she created Addams insisted that the social worker should remain offstage rather than step forward to the footlights—acting more like a modern business consultant.

What made Mother Cabrini so provoking to Jane Addams was that she seemed to have no need of that reserve.

Frances Cabrini began as a lay teacher in a small Italian town. Her youthful petitions to become a nun had been twice rejected; the church wanted her to work outside the monastic framework. She conformed little to the stereotype of the simple good nun. Cabrini suffered from lifelong depression and religious doubt; in 1883, she confessed in a letter that "neither in God nor my superiors do I find the comfort I need."[8] Action was her antidote to depression; her administrative skills seemed to fit her to organize a new venture in America, a ministry to the vast numbers of displaced, immigrant Italian peasants. She was finally received into an order of nuns with this goal in mind.

Mother Cabrini arrived in Chicago in 1889. Whatever her inner doubts, in the words of her biographer, the nun "was always a loyal daughter of the Church."[9] Her activities in American local church halls and parochial schools strictly followed rules laid down in Rome. Obedience to central authority led Mother Cabrini, through the Chicago Catholic newspaper *The New World*, to attack Hull House and Jane Addams as destructively permissive. *The New World* also attacked labor unions as dangerous instruments of socialist subversion, claiming that strikes defied the will of God. The church would not admit compassion as a purely neighborly experience, nor was compassion grounds for revolt.

The educational attainments of Catholic schools soon out-stripped those of Chicago's public schools; mutual aid societies organized by the church proved far stronger than those organized by the settlement houses. Traces of this strict, hierarchical regime indeed remained into my childhood in the project named for Mother Cabrini. Many of my neighbors, including Gloria Hayes, went to a school run by nuns, who continued Mother Cabrini's insistence that discipline and order were the essentials of education, rather than cooperative participation on the Hull House model. And though Jane Addams loathed the connection between hierarchy and compassion, she was fair-minded enough to recognize that at least in education the church regime worked.

More troubling to Addams, though less material, was the language of compassion which Mother Cabrini spoke. Addams was truly one of Marx's daughters in her dislike of religious ecstasy; it seemed a way to sweep a number of worldly evils under the tent of religious faith. Mother Cabrini spoke indeed about God's love in the same breath as the need for submission, but in doing so she elicited strong affection from all the immigrants her charities served: Polish and Irish as well as Italian. There may be a theological as well as personal explanation for this. The religious language of sin applies equally to all human beings, it does not single out and stigmatize the poor.

Addams, a believer in democratic participation, was condemned to silence about her care for others. Having removed compassion from the realm of sentimentality, she had made it inarticulate—and that silence had political consequences. She knew that simply to call the Catholic regime "paternalistic" would fall on deaf ears, especially the ears of those whom the regime was doing real good. But discretion does not arouse the masses.

Though rooted in Chicago, Addams was a secular cosmopolitan; she believed, like other settlement-house advocates, that the settlement house provided a model for social participation which could be applied across the differences of nations, races, or ethnic groups. Mother Cabrini instead focused in her charitable organizations on one particular problem of social difference, the dual identity of the immigrant. As she wrote late in her life, she wanted to train young immigrants "so that they will not be ashamed to be Italians," yet will "prove to their country of adoption that Italian migration is not a dangerous element."[10] Without hierarchical guidance, the poor immigrant had no means to keep these two forces in balance.

Perhaps the nun and the socialist could never have understood each other. Addams's coolness seemed to Mother Cabrini simply a kind of middle-class arrogance just as Hull House seemed to her an instrument of socialist subversion. Set in the raw capitalism of industrial Chicago, the Catholic elements of compassion—pity, humility, and sin—seemed to Jane Addams nearly obscene: they would lead only to more resignation and passivity of the sort which afflicted Italian peasants at home.

The New World itself represented one pole of a great conflict within the Catholic Church: is Christian socialism a contradiction in terms? To Mother Cabrini and her followers, it had to be, because socialism seemed the enemy of social order. To the next generation of Catholic service workers, like Dorothy Day and others in the Catholic Worker Movement, socialism

accorded with the spiritual impulses of voluntary poverty, identification with the weak and oppressed, which transcended
church hierarchy. Here lay a conundrum for the Catholic left
throughout the twentieth century, in Latin America as well as
in the United States. Radical clerics tried to be, at the same
time, guiding shepherds and self-effacing consultants.

The philosopher Natan Sznaider writes that there can be no
"compassion . . . without solidarity."[11] The origins of social work
show, on the contrary, the ambiguous relations between compassion and solidarity. Submission of the Catholic sort advo-
cated by Mother Cabrini made for solidarity of an explicit sort—
"we are all God's subjects"—and care could therefore be freely
expressed. More democratic forms of solidarity tend to be more
hesitant, less spontaneous; questions of inequality intrude.
Solidarity with the poor, if one is not poor, risks condescension,
or even more basically, the question of whether one has a legitimate place among those who are poor or deprived. Since solidarity is troubled by inequality, the declaration "I want to help"
can easily arouse a hostile response; or the person making this
declaration can hear it echoing without any response, like words
spoken into a well.

It was this ambiguity of solidarity among unequals which
troubled social workers like Jane Addams—or later, my
mother. The motives of the social workers were indeed frequently subject to misinterpretation; Addams was attacked by
many in the American labor movement as a subversive—else
why was she spending all her time in the slums?

In Chicago, the problematic relation between compassion
and solidarity historically preceded the tensions within the civil
rights movement and provided a frame for the disturbed rela-

tions between whites and blacks. Like Mother Cabrini, those who cooperated in the name of a shared religion had a resource to bridge this ambiguous divide between self and other: service to a higher power let them cross. But between blacks and Jews, between secular individuals, sheer social differentiation was harder to bridge.

Because the experience of caregiving is easier within hierarchical organizations than in democratic ones, conservatives are prone to argue that hierarchical caregiving is superior in its contents—the rules, duties, and conduct of all parties are clear. This is to argue that what is easiest is best. More informal forms of caregiving are indeed a struggle, just because equality itself has proved a disruptive force in modern society. Egalitarian dogmas of solidarity proved one of the great touchstones for social repression, from the French Revolution onward. This danger could hardly argue for a continuation of the *ancien régime,* but those who have sought to translate an idealogy of equality into compassionate acts have been most challenged by equality's political perils; they have been forced to confront the harm they might do to people unequal economically or socially to themselves.

My mother well expressed this difficulty when she explained her desire to practice social work as a "feeling that somewhere, quite close, but just out of reach, significant things were happening." The key phrase in this passage is "just out of reach."

Largesse and Caritas

Altruism, some biologists argue, is programmed into human genes. Like other social animals, we would perish if we did not

cooperate, if we did not give as well as take. But the act of giving needn't in itself carry the positive charge of a cooperative
act. Giving to others can be a way of manipulating them, or it
can serve the more personal need to affirm something in ourselves. Giving as a form of manipulation falls, in the history of
Western charity, into the category of largesse; the more personal and reflexive form of giving falls into the Christian category of caritas.

Jean Starobinski traces the Anglo-French word "largesse"
back to the Latin roots *largitio* and *largus*, implying an over-
flowing state of abundance.[12] Georges Bataille sees largesse as
Nature's abundance, like the overwhelming, nourishing light
depicted in Mexican myths, and again he imagines largesse as a
wealth human beings cannot possessively control, and "like a
river flowing into the sea, it must escape and be lost to us."[13] Jean-
Paul Sartre turned Bataille's image to political account, arguing
that the good society is a post-scarcity society. For Wordsworth,
largesse of spirit need not imply worldly riches. Wordsworth contrasts to those who simply perform the duty of charity his poor
neighbor who gives freely to a Cumberland beggar:

> . . . though pressed herself
> By her own wants, she from her store of meal
> Takes one unsparing handful for the scrip
> of this old Mendicant . . .[14]

In all these usages, largesse stands for generosity. They are
positive impulses; largesse of spirit means the impulse to *provide*, a simple, natural, and altruistic act.

Yet largesse contains the capacity to manipulate and corrupt others. Suetonius describes the Roman emperor Nero indulging in an orgy of largesse:

> Every day all kinds of gifts were thrown to the people. These included a thousand birds of every kind each day, various kinds of food, tickets for grain, clothing, gold, silver, precious stones, pearls, paintings, slaves, beasts of burden, even trained wild animals. . . .[15]

Artaud imagines the emperor Heliogabalus "feeding a castrated people. . . . Sperm, rose wines, embalming oils and the most expensive perfumes surround Heliogabalus's generosity with limitless irrigation."[16] And it was from such ancient examples that La Boétie made the connection between largesse and slavish submission: "Tyrants would distribute largesse . . . and then everybody would shamelessly cry 'Long Live the King!' "[17]

The master image which has organized Starobinski's own reflections on largesse, however, is a drawing by Correggio in the Louvre, one of the painter's most relaxed, the lines flowing and full without any seeming calculation. The drawing depicts a woman reaching out with a gift to a figure beyond the left edge, her face positioned at the upper right, full of serene love; this figure is Eve offering Adam the poisoned apple.

The two sides of largesse embody two extremes in the act which is at the heart of any welfare system: making a gift. At the one extreme is a gift freely given, at the other is the manipulative gift. The first embodies that aspect of character focused on the sheer fact that others lack something, that they are in need; the other act of giving uses it only as a means to gain power over them—as in Correggio's version of Eve, who offers a seductive present.

Christian writers conceived of the act of giving in altogether another form. Caritas means becoming a good person through making gifts; the act of giving combats one's own disposition to sinfulness. The value of the gift is irrelevant and even, in some versions, whether the gift does others good is irrelevant. This inward-turning state is often puzzling to non-Christians.

Prominent among modern non-Christians puzzled by caritas was the political philosopher Hannah Arendt. Arendt first wrote about caritas in 1929 in a youthful essay on Augustine. It was hardly a work of scholarly neutrality; like Jane Addams, Arendt thought Christian ethics stood in the way of social reform. The comparison between the two women is close; Arendt was also a social worker for several years, employed by Zionist organizations to deal with the problems of refugees fleeing Hitler's regime in the 1930s. Addams criticized the social hierarchy contained in Catholic charity; Arendt worried about basic tenets of Christianity itself. She approached social work with mental reservations that were due in part to the thinking she had done about St. Augustine.

St. Augustine conceived of love for one's neighbor in a way quite foreign to harboring warm feelings for any particular neighbor. Instead the Christian philosopher believed that "I love something in him . . . which, of himself, he is not," as Arendt paraphrases a passage from his *Confessions*.[18] The neighbor is someone whom we should see only in relation to God, not as a particular person. Again in Arendt's elegant formulation: "The Christian can love all people because each one is only an occasion, . . . the enemy and even the sinner . . . mere occasions for love. It is not really the neighbor who is loved in this love of neighbor—it is love itself."[19] The telling phrase here is that others become "mere occasions." Caritas involves knowing love rather than knowing you.

It should be said that modesty, so important to Christian ethics, is absent in her account, modesty of the sort which Jesus counsels in the Sermon on the Mount:

> Take heed that ye do not your alms before men, to be seen of them.... When thou doest alms, let not thy left hand know what thy right hand doeth: That thine alms may be in secret....[20]

But Arendt is not making a crude argument like Nathaniel Hawthorne's, that "benevolence is the twin of pride." What she wants to challenge is the Christian desire to transform oneself through giving.

In the desert of the world as the Christian feels it—so sterile, so empty—compassion fills up an absence in the self. Becoming a good person is in this sense reflexive and self-involved; without compassion, we are nothing, vacuous. Augustine himself says, "I have become a question to myself."[21] Developing one's capacity to give helps answer the question of what's potentially inside. Of course, in our sinful state, giving combats greed, but in the Sermon on the Mount, and throughout Matthew's Gospel, the act of giving appears as something more, the act which makes it possible to explore becoming a different sort of person. Measuring how much one's gift is worth to others is both venal and beside the point.

The practical direction in which Arendt is heading is clear: no modern welfare state should operate on Christian principles of this sort. The purpose of welfare is to do the recipient good; the feelings of the caregiver should be irrelevant. It's one reason why Arendt, when I came to know her as an elderly philosopher, spoke so acidly about her former profession; she thought social workers were a tribe bent on self-therapy, and they couldn't answer the question "Why are you helping me?" without giving that self-involvement away. The best kind of social welfare, she imagined, would be an accounting transaction involving no subjective relations.

Whether an accurate account or not, Arendt's reaction to St. Augustine should make us pause to define a basic principle for any secular welfare state: caregiving without compassion. What could this mean?

Caring for Others Without Compassion

Today, Arendt's position is taken by a vigorous if varied band of welfare reformers who subscribe to various versions of "basic incomes policy." All are moved, I think, by the belief that the state should give people the money they need to conduct their lives and then let them get on with their lives as they see fit.

The simplest form in which this can happen is to provide young people with a sum of money to be used for education or for purchase of a house, or simply to be saved for later use. This is the proposition put forward by the American jurist Bruce Ackerman, and now enacted into law in Great Britain. More radical proposals envision true income support. The Dutch welfare reformer Van Pariij and the German sociologist Claus Offe argue that the state should provide an income to all citizens sufficient to let them purchase education and health care if they wish to do so; the basic income continues throughout a person's life, and so replaces state pensions. In the most radical version, everyone gets a basic income grant, regardless of whether he or she needs it; "means testing" disappears.[22]

Without getting into the economics of these proposals (the numbers turn out, for Britain and Germany at least, to be persuasive, since welfare budgets including unemployment support shrink radically), their social logic is striking. Unlike liberal welfare reform, these proposals envision a strong dependence on the state for financial assistance. But like liberal welfare reform they imagine doing away with any emotional assistance, minimizing the subjective sides of dependency in the welfare state—for there is no longer "welfare" as a face-to-face human interaction. The gift is no longer a personal gift; you would have to thank the Treasury's computers.

What would it mean socially to remove compassion from the act of providing care? The proposals of Ackerman and Offe don't envision absolute equality, rather the elimination of material neediness. They believe that this guarantee would make people more social equals, and so strengthen the possibility for truly mutual respect. The closest real-world analogues to this are Scandinavian societies in the mid-twentieth-century era when their welfare states were intact.

I want to believe them, but the experience of my hand injury stands in the way. I wanted at the time of my surgery to have a human being take responsibility for it, to know the name of my doctor, to know him; my life is not a function. And when the operation on my hand went wrong, I wanted it to matter to the doctor. The failure of his skill should have prompted him to some soul-searching about himself, as in fact it did.

Impersonal caregiving is a very pessimistic view of the human condition; it supposes people are likely to do others injury by caring for and about them personally, so that the human elements of judgment and response to need should be eliminated. But would my hand surgeon, if he did not know my name, if he did not know I was a musician, if I was only a hand, would he under these conditions have any compelling motive to reexamine his own practices, his own skill?

Arendt herself, I think, didn't grasp the kind of self-searching and self-transformation Augustine had in mind. It can be conveyed in purely secular terms by thinking about the mourning of a death. Mourning begins with an overwhelming sense of personal loss. In the course of time, however, the mourner will feel that the love felt for one person can be transferred to another; equally, the mourner will realize what the loss of someone leaves inside: knowing love itself. This is mourning as an unfolding process, as a narrative; love detaches itself from the beloved, love remains.

The divorce of caregiving from compassion, bred by her reading of St. Augustine, was crucial in setting Arendt on the path of her own political convictions. Again like Jane Addams, she came particularly to loathe charity given in the name of pity. Pity for the poor, the weak, or the infirm carries an undertow of contempt; Arendt refused to credit the theology which moved Mother Cabrini, the Christian view of all men and women as equal sinners. For Arendt the loathing of pity had a specifically Jewish framework. The Zionism to which Arendt subscribed as a young woman remained with her the rest of her life. She hoped that if they regained Palestine, Jews would no longer be treated as objects of pity, as victims—even though eventually she became a critic of the Jewish state's treatment of Palestinians.

Her youthful critique of Augustinian doctrines also colored Arendt's relation to feminism; feminism seemed just more of the self-involvement and self-searching she perceived in Christian acts of compassion. The feminism of her time in America was often indeed of the confessional, consciousness-raising variety, and this activity little suited her tastes. But the relation of subjective compassion and gender is much too important to leave at this.

Arendt's critique is blind to the presence of Mary in Augustine's thoughts. In the Middle Ages, Marian cults prompted caregiving during plague epidemics when self-interest would have dictated only separation from other people. Plagues were largely urban phenomena, and people even in that prescientific age knew they should flee cities in order to save themselves; the Marian cults kept them in the streets, nursing the sick, disposing of dead bodies, strewing bundles of supposedly health-giving herbs outside buildings—compassionate acts that only increased the death toll.

The image of Mary was a double one, the historian Caroline Bynam says, one image being of a mother who freely gives her care, the other of a mother overwhelmed by grief at the killing of her son. This second image was as important as the first in the annals of compassion. St. Augustine and the other early church fathers had preached a doctrine of the "alien body of Christ," God's suffering unfathomable by ordinary people. The popular movements of the Middle Ages founded on the "imitation of Christ" were modeled on Mary's grief, and supposed that ordinary people could empathetically feel Christ's physical sufferings, so drawing closer to Him, and by extension drawing close to one another. The result, Georges Duby maintains, is that Christianity came "to have every appearance of being a people's religion," binding the community together.[23]

In these popular Christian movements, compassion was "gendered" yet included both men and women. While classic liberalism has felt something akin to a horror of the primal maternal scene, modern feminist psychologists have sought to follow something of the Marian thread, though their language seems at first to break it. For under present arrangements, they argue, women follow a different developmental path from men in the experience of compassion.

This is the spirit in which Nancy Chodorow asserts that "girls emerge [from adolescence] with a stronger basis for experiencing another's needs or feelings as one's own," so that what I've called character would seem to be a character reserved for women. Chodorow claims that because girls "are parented by a person of the same gender," they "come to experience themselves as less differentiated than boys, as more continuous with and related to the external object-world."[24] Carol Gilligan asserts that "women not only define themselves in a context of human relationship but also judge themselves in terms of their ability to care."[25]

As stereotypes these assertions would be meaningless; many women simply aren't like this. But the two writers are arguing that feminine compassion stands for a developmental possibility. When either a man or a woman emerges from childhood highly sensitive to others, his or her character then is labeled by society as feminine.

Arendt would not have accepted this, because her youthful critique of caritas began a lifelong search to envisage a public realm freed of questions of self; like many of her basic-income heirs, she believed the human psyche was largely a source of collective misrule. In *On Revolution* she argued that modern politics is crippled by psychology; what counts instead is solidarity among strangers. The "love of the world" came to figure frequently as an image in her writings, but she meant by that "love" something completely opposite from what St. Augustine or Carol Gilligan meant. As two commentators on her last essay, *Willing,* have put it, love of the world meant "an internal binding force with no apparent external mediation," implying neither self nor God.[26]

Caring without compassion may seem so cold and heartless a version of mutual respect that perhaps it's not amiss to cite an incident the writer Mary McCarthy reports in her correspondence with the philosopher. In 1970, three weeks after Arendt's husband had died, the poet W. H. Auden suddenly proposed marriage to her. His own life had run aground in pills and drink, and he had been abandoned by his longtime lover Chester Kallman. Arendt rejected him immediately. "I hate, am afraid of pity," she wrote to McCarthy, "and I think I never knew anyone who aroused my pity to this extent. . . . I refused to take care of him when he came and asked for shelter."[27] She is not cold; rather, she does not wish to look down on him. She does not wish her pity to breed disrespect for him as a man and a poet. Such respecting without loving was just the difficult problem Jane Addams faced.

Perhaps as a coda to caring for others without compassion, we might want to consider what is commonly called "compassion fatigue."

Compassion Fatigue

"Compassion fatigue" stands for the exhaustion of our sympathies in the face of persistently painful realities—victims of torture, masses of people wiped out by plague, the sheer scale of the Holocaust make so many demands on our emotions that eventually we stop feeling. Like a fire, compassion burns out.

Compassion fatigue is also often cited by critics of the therapeutic welfare state as a reason to look for more impersonal arrangements. There is a compelling logic in this view, as anyone who has worked in voluntary organizations can attest. Over the course of time, volunteers burn out from too much stress, from too many demands on their emotions. In a later part of this book, I'll present some statistics on the turnover of volunteers; here we need to take note of some suspicions which the phenomenon of compassion fatigue arouses.

The sociologist Stanley Cohen, for instance, has studied compassion fatigue in public responses to victims of torture. He observes that torture victims, rather than eliciting an exhausting excess of response, may arouse in those who watch or listen to their stories a fear of identifying at all. He notes that people routinely watch and enjoy the infliction of physical pain in films, but can't bear to face real torture. Cohen contrasts them to a doctor who cannot let himself go to pieces whenever a patient dies; the doctor faces a truly overwhelming reality, and needs reserve as self-protection, in order to keep on operating.[28]

The phrase "compassion fatigue" prompts a perhaps more universal question—how much regard are other people due? This question lurks in all issues having to do with subjective engagement—in the limits of concern we might feel for the difficulties another person faces in a job, as much as sympathy for physical pain. To say that people are due as much attention as possible is no answer at all. At some point everyone declares, "I've reached my limit," or "You have no right to expect more."

The reception of a famous painting by Brueghel poses this question of limits; the painting is his *Landscape with the Fall of Icarus*. It shows the young Icarus plunging from the sky into the sea, though at first sight, it is hard to tell that this is a painting about Icarus at all. Brueghel depicts nothing of the story of Icarus—the young man's donning of wax wings so that he can fly, the melting of the wax as Icarus soars up toward the sun. Only his two legs are shown as he splashes into the water, a small detail on the canvas. By contrast, Brueghel has boldly designed and painted in vivid colors a pastoral scene of a farmer plowing his fields, a shepherd tending his sheep, a fisherman casting; beyond them, in the bay, a ship sails toward a city spread out in the far distance. People go about their daily rounds, unmindful of the drama which has unfolded in their midst.

To the poet W. H. Auden, Brueghel had dramatized sheer indifference to real suffering, which Stanley Cohen calls "seeing but not seeing." Auden's interpretation of the painting is this:

> In Brueghel's *Icarus*, for instance: how everything turns away
> Quite leisurely from the disaster; the ploughman may
> Have heard the splash, the forsaken cry,
> But for him it was not an important failure; the sun shone
> As it had to on the white legs disappearing into the green
> Water; and the expensive delicate ship that must have seen
> Something amazing, a boy falling out of the sky,
> Had somewhere to get to and sailed calmly on.[29]

But others have seen something different; the figures in Brueghel's painting may simply have been realists. A Dutch proverb of the time declared: "No plow is stopped for the sake of a dying man."[30] Had the farmer stopped tilling the soil, the ship broken its course, they could hardly have saved the drowning boy; it would have done no good.

So the aversion people feel to acknowledging pain could be given a less negative cast. Sensitivity to the sufferings of others would disrupt people from getting on with the business of life; there's suffering enough in just seeking to survive. Only saints, perhaps, could respond so freely to a boy trying to fly.

This commonsense interpretation of the painting leaves out perhaps its most striking visual element: there is no sign of suffering in it. The painter does not display the terror of Icarus; the painting makes no demand for pity. The viewer has to intuit that something is radically amiss from almost imperceptible details, which in themselves would mean nothing without knowledge of the mythological story. What Brueghel has presented the viewer somewhat resembles the problem posed by people in pain who keep it to themselves; they too oblige others to fill in, to interpret.

In everyday life indifference is often checked socially by the same experience one has looking at the painting: something indeed doesn't seem quite right, and one begins to puzzle why. There is a certain freedom in this arousal, something St. Augustine elaborated on in the concept of caritas; it is a noticing that things are not as they should be, and in that regard lies the germ of compassion. But this interpretative act also poses a danger. Unprompted, freely made, there are no limits to what one might find, the rottenness and suffering one might discover; there is the risk of losing control over what one might find, and so feel. "Compassion fatigue" is a kind of premonition of this arousal leading to loss of control.

Sociologically, hierarchical regimes free the expression of compassion from this danger, by removing the element of free discovery and interpretation. Only when rules, commands, and obligations are repressed in the name of freedom does compassion risk become unmanageable. This is why disaster-care programs which rely on volunteers frequently run aground, once the first impulse to help passes; relief workers become overwhelmed by their own reactions.

What is true of compassion is true more largely of the acts of recognition and regard which orchestrate the experience of respect. As a free act, generated by subjective interpretation, respect for others can become wearing just because it would possess no limits, no boundaries. It's this oppressive possibility which makes the conflict between the nun and the socialist a durable parable. If hierarchy is, as Jane Addams thought, the wrong way to give social shape to a person's powers of interpretation, then what alternative social forms could relieve the subjective burden which lurks in freely and openly responding to others?

Lagresse complicates any answer, because it demonstrates the munipulative power of gift-giving. Even the freely given gift can injure the self-respect of the person to whom it is given, for "charity wounds," as the anthropologist Mary Douglas says; it lays a heavy burden of gratitude on the recipient, who may have nothing to give back but submission. When compassion takes the form of pity, it also can demean the receiving party. "Compassion may itself be a substitute for justice," Arendt argues, since pity "always signifies inequality."[31] This is the argument against largesse.

For these reasons, some strategists of welfare reform have tried to imagine the provision of care divorced from sentiments of compassion. They do not want the provision of care to succumb when compassion burns out. There may be indeed something unnatural—fit only for saints—about responding freely to pain, more than the conduct of everyday life obliges. This is the argument against caritas.

And yet. Like my relations with the hand surgeon, most people cannot accept the provision of care as a neutral function.

Part Three

An Argument
About Welfare

Reformers of the welfare state are sociologists of a sort. They believe work to be a better source of self-respect than a government check; they believe institutions and professionals should be replaced wherever possible by communities and volunteers. Behind these social aspirations lies the belief that the welfare state should operate more like a profit-making business.

Reform of this sort is naive sociology. Naive because the complications of talent, dependence, and caregiving cannot be erased by privatization or community care; moreover, the reformers' view of social institutions themselves is faulty. To act on this faulty knowledge only exaggerates inequalities of respect, disconnecting welfare clients from the rest of society.

Chapter Six

Bureaucratic Respect

Homeless Adolescents

By 1975, I could travel through Cabrini only in a car, and that only during the day; the community had become too dangerous. Twice I did so with a pair of beleaguered black policemen; their superiors looked on them as soft, since they did not treat residents of the projects as inevitable enemies. The policemen knew the community well and could accurately catalog and classify the young people who lived there.

Off the streets, the Robert Taylor Homes next to Cabrini had produced another young doctor. Perhaps his achievement was even more remarkable than the eye surgeon's; as an adolescent, this doctor had been homeless for several months. Sometime in his middle teens he had fled a family in which both the father and mother were on drugs, and he was rescued from squatting in abandoned apartments only when taken in by an orphanage.

On the streets, the cops pointed to less fortunate homeless

youths. There were young men who had committed crimes, been sent to juvenile reformatories, and then returned home but not to their families. These kids looked tough, but others pointed out to me did not: kids who had fled physical violence or drugs at home or fled because they were on drugs. Juvenile homelessness in and around the project had, the police said, become increasingly evident—whereas homeless children were rare in Cabrini during my youth.

Few of those the cops pointed out were homeless in the sense that term is usually deployed—that is, sleeping outside. The welfare system did a good job of bringing youngsters without any refuge, who would have died of the cold of Chicago winters, into shelter. The larger homeless population survived more as squatters, colonizing vacant apartments in the project or floating from friend to friend.

Homelessness is not just an affliction of individuals; it happens to families, and for many reasons, economic as well as social. Based on census figures, the most expert estimate is that about 1 percent of the population of the United States experience homelessness during the course of a year. More than half of homeless families consist of single mothers with children less than four years old. It's difficult to make precise comparisons with other countries about families; for juveniles, one recent estimate for both Britain and Germany is about forty thousand runaways or abandoned children in any one year.[1] Juvenile homelessness is, statistically, an extreme problem suffered by a relatively small but not insignificant number of people.

In the 1970s, the institutions which tried to work with this floating population began to change. Few new orphanages had been created in Chicago after the Second World War, and the system of foster parentage was under attack; paid foster parents often lacked the skills to deal with drug-addicted youngsters, or equally, to deal with the consequences of the child abuse which had driven many youngsters to flee their own parents.

"Deinstitutionalization" was the policy buzzword of those years, with a corresponding emphasis on "care in the community." The idea of removing children from the community had fallen under attack in analyses such as Erving Goffman's *Asylums* (1961) or Peter Townsend's *The Last Refuge* (1962), works which indicted residential care for the elderly, for mental patients, and for children as "total institutions," rigid bureaucracies more like prisons than refuges.[2] By the end of the 1970s this attack would be consummated in Michel Foucault's *Discipline and Punish,* in which inmates were portrayed as deprived of a sense of self, and so of self-respect, by the invasive powers of residential or corrective institutions.[3]

The closure of asylums, reform schools, and public geriatric homes proceeded faster than the provision of resources to communities. Moreover, the belief that community could replace residential care overlooked a necessary symbiosis between the two domains. In foster care for children, for instance, the children need somewhere to live in between placements; one British study estimated that to maintain 38,000 children in foster care, 2,850 residential places in children's homes were necessary each year.[4] But the government advocates of deinstitutionalism ignored such symbiosis in the effort to reduce costs and responsibilities.

Deinstitutionalism had a wider scope, however, than the desire of mean-fisted legislators to save money. The most famous of all reforms of this kind, Law No. 180, passed by the Italian

government in 1979, came as a result of pressure from the Left
to end the true horrors which prevailed in many Italian mental
asylums; moreover, a sufficient sum of money was provided to
localities to pay for social workers and doctors in the community. But even with these resources it proved difficult to keep in
contact with patients outside asylum walls. The complex needs
of former patients didn't cease when they were given their freedom; the number of homeless and disoriented people on the
streets—appropriately called *abbandonati*—dramatically
increased. Social workers had to reinvent, so to speak, the
bureaucratic wheel.[5]

In Chicago, as in other American cities, the practice of dein-
stitutionalizing children encountered a further difficulty
because of the high rates of parental abuse in the United States.
A recent study of forty thousand homeless and runaway children reveals that 8 percent of the girls experienced sexual abuse
in the home, compared to 2 percent of the boys; physical abuse
was suffered by 16 percent of the boys and 20 percent of the
girls; parental neglect (principally failure to provide food, but
also leaving a child alone unsupervised for more than seven
days) occurred among 20 percent of the boys and 18 percent of
the girls.[6] These children had fled believing they were safer
homeless; they often flee their local communities as well as their
families; they are children particularly difficult to reach in
casual contacts with social workers, since they tend to keep their
histories of abuse—especially sexual abuse—to themselves.

Community care practices for juvenile offenders on the
streets are perhaps the thorniest of all the issues posed by deinstitutionalization. The numbers of young people from places
like Cabrini who go to jail has radically increased in the last

four decades. In America, this increase represents crimes committed in order to obtain or sell drugs; in both Britain and America, the jails also fill up because of what John Pitts calls the "dejuvenilization" of justice, the application of adult sentencing standards to youthful offenders.[7] Communities themselves have hardened against potential or prior offenders; ghetto residents want to "take back the streets" from criminals and bad behavior. The desire is well expressed in a document prepared by leaders of Britain's Labour Party in 1996:

> This greater emphasis on discipline [legally] should be matched in the local community. Excessive tolerance of low-level sub-criminal behavior by unruly young people undermines general respect for the rule of law, ruins the environment and makes a misery of the lives of many innocent people. . . .[8]

The former juvenile offender is caught in a vise. The presumption is that he or she will offend again. The services to prevent that outcome have diminished; Chicago has not been alone in reducing the resources available for parole work with juveniles. Homelessness compounds the difficulty of "going straight" in the community, since the ex-offender easily disappears from view. Voluntary work with homeless juveniles has dramatically increased in the last generation, particularly in the United States, Britain, and the Netherlands. But these voluntary workers are discovering that they too cannot do without some sustaining institutional frame; the turnover in volunteers tends to be high, and weekly contacts with kids in need is not enough to provision their daily support.

The deinstitutionalization of welfare signals a broader change in modern society: an attack on rigid institutions in work and in politics. As in welfare, so in this broader effort the commanding belief is that communities can meet people's social needs better than bureaucracies. And as in welfare, communities are thereby tested; they frequently cannot meet those needs.

The Bureaucratic Pyramid

Though the phrase "rigid bureaucracy" seems to denote an inherent evil, there was a good reason for the rise of rigid institutions in both work and the welfare state, one which goes back to the initial terrors and confusions of industrial capitalism.

Those alarms are evident in the novels of the nineteenth century, such as Balzac's *Lost Illusions*. He portrays, for instance, David, a good craftsman who cannot organize the knowledge of his hands into a large-scale industry. Balzac's readers also lacked practical knowledge of how to make institutions efficient. It puzzled many managers that the more minutely they divided up the work in an office, the less productive the office became—a conundrum, for instance, in French banks and American importing firms. In the figure of financier Melmotte in *The Way We Live Now,* Trollope created a man who understands his own money but not the logic of international banks; Trollope's readers understood the ways of leveraged investment no better. The center of the new capitalism, the city, was itself illegible; looking in 1906 at the burgeoning skyscrapers shooting up in New York, Henry James thought they resembled "pins in a cushion already over-planted, and stuck as in the dark, anywhere and anyhow."[9]

A welfare state as we understand it did not exist under these conditions: no old-age pensions, medical insurance, safety standards, unemployment benefits, or universal schooling; such help as people in need received came from private, voluntary acts of charity. One problem in this burgeoning capitalism did, however, stimulate debates about state protection: child labor, which was as grinding in London in the 1830s as it is in the Third World today. "Reform" in that era focused on protecting children at work.

The absence of the welfare state was in part due to the lack of organizational structure which afflicted capitalism's critics and enemies. Trade unions were small; the most common form of industrial protest was the local wildcat strike or work stoppage, erupting and ceasing suddenly. Not until the century's end could trade-union and socialist leaders define whom they were leading, and to what end.

For all these reasons, as late as 1938, looking back, the then MP Harold Macmillan reflected, "Nobody ever *invented* capitalist society," arguing that free-market competition produced no institutional order.[10]

The disorganization of early capitalism produced a code of self-respect and mutual esteem riddled with contradictions. Society in part still lay in the shadows of the *ancien régime*, a society in which social position was sharply defined, and within state, army, and church there was a ladder to climb. Stendhal evokes the shadow cast by this old regime in *The Red and the Black*, whose protagonist, Julien Sorel, quickly learns how to readjust his clothing, his speech, and his bodily comportment each time he takes a step up.

Looking around him, however, Julien Sorel perceived these

were no more than shadows; the driven and the greedy could bludgeon their way up, and no customs or manners could protect them if they fell. Sorel suffered therefore from anomie, in the form defined by the sociologist Emile Durkheim as "rulelessness," the experience of someone in free fall, disoriented.

The historian Robert Wiebe has thus called the late nineteenth century's reaction to the anarchies of capitalism a "search for order," composed equally of structuring institutions and shaping social connections.[11] The talent hierarchies of the eighteenth century provided one model, but these were not broad enough in scope to serve. The order-making institution had to include those who would go nowhere as well as those who would rise. They had to provision welfare of some sort in order to quell revolt against misery. First and foremost, however, the order-making institution had to protect big businesses from the free market.

The capitalists of the 1880s and 1890s had made a simple discovery: the markets of their time were inimical to amassing profits. The difficulty lay not simply in the lack of regulation of stock markets. In infrastructure projects like the building of railroads, a large number of stakeholders made it difficult to plan coherently and to accumulate investment capital; profits had equally to be parceled out. In the 1880s and 1890s, capitalists began to seek, therefore, protection from competition; trusts like Rockefeller's Standard Oil Corporation sought to absorb their competitors, or destroy them by forcing prices to levels below the cost of production. In manufacturing, profits could be effectively increased by eliminating independent suppliers.

Just to put some numbers to this consolidation: from 1881 to 1929, the average size of businesses in the United States rose from six to eighty-four employees; firms of more than ten thousand employees appeared for the first time. In this same period, as a measure of stability, the longevity of medium-sized businesses tripled, while the longevity of businesses with fewer than ten employees was cut in half. Market competition, as measured by variation in the cost of household goods, diminished, as the number of producers became ever fewer.[12] From the end of the First World War to the 1970s, businesses were consolidated throughout Western Europe as in North America; the impulse was to combine operations rather than split them up.

This change contained another: as the size of firms increased, so did the power of bureaucrats staffing them. Weber summed up the power of administrators in a short essay written at the end of his career:

> In a modern state real *rule* becomes effective in everyday life neither through parliamentary speeches nor through the pronouncements of monarchs but through the day-to-day management of the administration; it necessarily and inevitably lies in the hands of officialdom, both military and civilian.[13]

The comparison between civilian and military organization is revealing. In escaping the market, corporations began to function more like armies. Specifically, they devised a clear chain of command, so that orders devised by a few people at the top could be transmitted to the masses below. It's in this military model for capitalism that the phenomenon of rigid bureaucracy makes its modern appearance.

If Standard Oil exemplified the desire to flee the anarchy of markets, the Ford Motor Works exemplified how military order could be imposed internally, within organizations. Ford was an enormous organization centralized in one place; it operated strictly through a hierarchical chain of command. In its obsessive attention to how workers spent each minute of the working day, the planners of the Ford Works sought to bring rigid order to a kind of apotheosis, one in which the company's leaders knew and directed exactly what everyone in the giant organization was doing at any given moment.[14]

The comparison between army and corporation crystallizes in the image of the bureaucratic pyramid. The image is so familiar that its radical import is easy to miss. It can assert raw power over talent and merit—economically, as when Rockefeller crushed profitable competitors; they were not to be given the chance to show what they could do. In its internal rigidity, the bureaucratic pyramid can also crush individual enterprise and intelligence—famously so in the mind-numbing routines of the Ford Motor Works. Equally, however, the bureaucratic pyramid is not a soulless machine; it defines social relations of a particular sort.

As in armies, so in businesses, "leadership" has a charismatic rather than purely functional quality. The oft-made comparison between Napoleon and John D. Rockefeller is in this way a precise one: both secretive men, neither explaining and justifying himself. Their commands were authoritative just because those below believed the leaders could see farther, understand what the followers could not; they were virtuosos. Though a bureaucratic pyramid seems the very embodiment of the division of labor, the business executive, like the high-ranking military officer, operates as a generalist, a comprehensive strategist. The division of labor does not apply to him or her; specialists in top jobs are simply too narrow-minded to lead. More, authority of this sort at the top affects the experience of dependence below: you submit believing that someone in command knows what he or she is doing.

Nor does a rigid organization grow quite efficiently. The number of soldiers or workers expands far more rapidly than niches for generals or bosses. Bureaucracy tends to sprawl by cellular division at the base, beyond the functional needs of the organization, as when three people do work one alone could perform. Weber, in observing the bottom-heavy bureaucracies of his time, explained sprawl simply as a consequence of the bureaucrat's own desire for power; like officers, bureaucrats want ever more people to command. But sprawl accomplishes one task of inclusion: places, if useless places, will be generated for ever larger numbers of people. Rockefeller's Standard Oil performed this task well; the destroyed competitors were often given desk jobs in which they could exercise little power but were pacified by their salaries.

Time is the most puissant force binding the rigid organization together socially. The longer people work in an organization, the more they get involved in its problems, its intrigues; the corporation becomes a kind of real-world theater. The institution provides in time what the sociologist Robert Michels called a *Lebensführung*, which in English might be rendered as "life narrative in an institution." This institutional narrative should, in principle, solve the problem of anomie posed by Durkheim; instead of the experience of free fall, of moving jerkily or aimlessly forward in time, the individual is given a sustained place in the world.

"Service" becomes the emblem of social honor in such organizations, but this emblem comes with a price. One's sense of an honorable place is not of one's own making.

• • • •

The origins of the "total institution" thus lie in the attempts begun a century ago to solve the illegibility and chaos of competitive capitalism. Blaming such institutions on the welfare state, as Goffman and Townsend do, misses their true origins and the economic hold they have exerted on modern society. Nor does identifying the total institution with capitalism reckon one great paradox of the twentieth century: the spread of Fordism and bureaucratic rigidity into the postrevolutionary, totalitarian world of state socialism. The formation of rigid bureaucracy during his lifetime Weber described as the creation of an "iron cage."[15] But this image is also somewhat misleading.

The iron cages of bureaucracy, whether capitalist or communist, could not have been built simply as prisons; they had to offer something to lure people inside. The bureaucratic *Lebensführung* satisfied a basic need for organizing one's life narrative; service to the institution could earn regard from others. By the 1950s, researchers studying the apotheosis of rigid bureaucracy—such as C. Wright Mills in *White Collar* or W. H. Whyte in *The Organization Man*—found employees thus intensely involved in the theater of corporate life as actors, not as spectators. Of course the institutions could make people unhappy, but the fact that the iron cage engaged its inmates helps explain the application of this bureaucratic model to the welfare state.

There was never any doubt among creators of the welfare state that comprehensive bureaucratic tools were needed to fix the capitalist machine. When the Great Depression of the 1930s began, only one in a hundred American workers had unemployment insurance, fewer than one in eight a retirement scheme, less than one in twenty health insurance; few British laborers had affordable access to hospitals, and almost none to universities.[16] In this regard, a misleading contrast is often drawn between the United States and Germany or Great Britain, the American welfare system seeming far weaker in its origins. In fact, as the sociologist Theda Skocpol has shown, Americans have long accepted the legitimacy of welfare machinery, in providing pension schemes—a legitimacy which can be traced back the pensions demanded by soldiers who had fought in the American Civil War.[17]

But the welfare state represents very different versions of the state. The sociologist Gösta Esping-Anderson divides these states into three kinds: the liberal welfare regime, which delivers state benefits parsimoniously to individuals; the social-democratic regime, which stresses universal entitlements to state help; and conservative welfare regimes, which try to channel state aid to families and localities rather than individuals. The development of the American welfare system after the Second World War represents the first regime, Scandinavian welfare the second, and Italian welfare the third.[18]

All these regimes, however, to some degree developed as public cartels and monopolies, in the sense that the state replaced irregular private charities, or provided services which the market had not generated. But the public and private sectors did not grow apart.

Economically, the private sector became deeply enmeshed in the welfare state—broadly conceived to include education, health, and pensions, as well as care of the poor. Ten million Americans currently work in health services, five million in private human services, five million in education and social work, eleven million in state and government services—about 22 percent of all employees.[19] No simple line separates non-profit and profit-seeking labor; most private hospitals depend, for instance, on government funds to cover their costs.

Moreover, the "state" in the welfare state is often assumed simply to be a national state. Even in countries which developed generous provisions, this assumption does not hold. In Sweden, one analyst notes that "20 county councils cover over 65% of total health-care expenditure through local income taxes, and are directly responsible for the management of almost all aspects of the health system."[20] In Germany, another seemingly centralized welfare state, the regional *Länder* have come to possess great control in health and education; local authorities fund 20 percent of total school expenditure.

But the social features of rigid bureaucracy in corporations and armies came, despite these twists, to apply to welfare pyramids. Charismatic leadership the least so; Bismarck in the nineteenth century, and Franklin Roosevelt in the twentieth stand out as people who led with authority, but the names of most of the creators of welfare states are known only to specialists.

The "careers" of institutionalized welfare clients, as Goffman called them, their life narratives in prisons and asylums, as single mothers on American AFDC programs, or as the permanently unemployed in Italy, are much more familiar social phenomena, and much more despised. Proliferation at the base of the welfare system has tokened not so much social inclusion as parasitism.

The most profound parallel between army, corporate, and welfare pyramids lies, however, in how people do feel socially included. In the army and in corporate life, esteem in the iron cage comes for service to the institution; approval is conferred by an institution upon an individual for belonging. In the welfare pyramid, something akin can occur, but is complicated by the circumstances of dependence.

My childhood was a world shaped by the bureaucratic pyramid. It embodied a welfare pyramid in the making; the Roosevelt era was the first in which "welfare" was expanded in scope to include massive public housing projects. The pyramid put in place removed tenants from the operations of the market; the regime that cared for them became ever thicker with bureaucratic rules and bureaucrats. A material need was met, but a nonmaterial need was addressed as well: for black tenants who had been treated with contempt down South, it mattered that the bureaucracy acknowledge them as persons.

Gloria Hayes Morgan, my childhood friend, writes: "Passing the Chicago Housing Authority's screening provided a seal of approval of sorts to families of modest means."[21] The thick rulebook determining who could live in the community, who could be awarded this "stamp of approval," contrasted not only to the American South, but to the conditions of unattached migrants to northern cities, who were treated, as the novelist Ralph Ellison put it, as "invisible men."

When William Whyte studied the middle-class denizens of big corporations in the same era I lived in Cabrini, he found the institutional "stamp of approval" mattered just as much; white-collar workers looked to the corporations to treat them as whole human beings. IBM, for instance, created training schools inside its walls, provided special access to health care and loans for

housing, built golf courses for employees. The result transformed employees into members of an institutional family.

Time was a powerful ingredient in producing this result.
People who stayed in Cabrini cared far more about the place
than those who passed through; the same was true at IBM.
Whyte found middle-level employees often critical of procedures, peers, and bosses; they spoke up because they had committed their lives to the institution. The most critical voices in
Cabrini were also to be found among long-term residents who
had become the most involved.

A classic explanation for why this happens comes from the
economist Albert Hirschmann. He sees in institutions a three-
cornered relation between loyalty, voice (which means just that,
speaking up), and exit (which means withdrawal from engagement, as well as physical departure). A long time spent in
pyramidal bureaucracies, he found, breeds a robust correlation
between loyalty and voice.[22] This correlation is just what Goffman, Foucault, and other critics of total institutions fear. They
are advocates of emotional "exit." Bureaucratic approval is a
danger to the free self.

If in its early days Cabrini commanded strong loyalty from
its black residents, a later generation in Cabrini regretted the
disintegration of bureaucratic control. After race riots in 1968
which burned out the homes of many poor people, the authorities simply shoved into the project anyone who needed shelter.
Rochelle Satchell, whose life spanned the good and bad times in
Cabrini, recalled:

> You had some girls and guys and all they wanted to do was
> fight. It was a nightmare. . . . The process that the Chicago

Housing Authority had used for screening families in order to move in here, [now there] was no screening, they was just putting families in.[23]

1968 was a defining moment for children in the project as well. Now a confluence of factors—broken homes, the surge in drugs, deinstitutionalization that returned adolescent criminals to their communities if not their homes, all coupled to a welfare regime which had ceased judging residents as worthy or not worthy of admission—combined to produce visible numbers of displaced or homeless kids on the street.

The changes in Cabrini from my generation to the next are not a brief for the virtues of rigid bureaucracy. Rather, they illustrate what is the real social power of such institutions: their capacity to regulate self-respect and communal respect by passing judgment and awarding approval to whole human beings. The image of big bureaucracy as soulless and impersonal, modeled on the Ford production line, does not quite fit the corporate world, and certainly does not adequately describe the experience of bureaucracy in welfare institutions.

Were welfare simply a cash transfer to those who need help, bureaucracy would not possess the power to regulate respect; the state would simply compute the money people need, give it to them, and leave them to fend for themselves. But accounting procedures seldom meet the specific demands of welfare; cash transfers would do little to help sexually abused homeless girls, or keep a housing project functioning as a community, or address the loneliness of elderly people parked in hospitals.

•   •   •

In the Cabrini of my generation, when the bureaucratic pyramid was firmly in place, strict regulations governed how the buildings could be used and appropriate behavior on the streets; a regime of surveillance led to intervention in family affairs, as after the glass wars. Cabrini was hardly unique in its regulative approach to how people should live. In Britain's Peabody Estates, tenants could not "sublet, take in washing, undertake out work, keep pets, paper their rooms, hang pictures on their walls or stay out after 11 p.m."; the front doors of the buildings were locked and the gas turned off each night to ensure the last provision.[24] A modern housing worker says of her relations to residents that she sees herself "as the person telling them how to be a tenant . . . being a good tenant . . . I see if the place has been cleaned . . . I check up on them."[25]

The middle-class parallels in the world of *The Organization Man* to these regulations were, for instance, the famous white shirts and dark suits required of all employees by IBM's dress code, or the prohibition in other corporations on owning foreign-made cars, or again and more gravely, the pressures put on homosexual employees to lie about their private lives.

In both the housing project and the corporation, the institution makes respectable the fact of dependency but does not honor autonomy within that relationship. The psychological possibility of combining dependency and autonomy envisioned by Erikson or Winnicott does not find organizational expression in such practices.

There is a psychological relationship built into welfare regimes like those of the United States which do not treat welfare as a right. Screening interviews or diagnostic profiles try to get behind the pretenses or silences which constitute people's public masks in order to know, if they really need help, what help they need. In my generation, the emphasis was on finding people in need, but soon this gave way to a more adversarial relation; as the country became richer, suspicion of those who remained poor increased.

It's not surprising, therefore, that the welfare analysts Richard Cloward and Frances Fox Piven have found American welfare recipients to complain of being treated with a lack of respect in the sense of being "got at," even when they prove themselves truly in need and "worthy" of help.[26] They are being judged as whole human beings—now an adversarial judgment in which the party judged feels naked.

That fear of being "got at" is what theorists of the total institution like Goffman and Foucault have picked up on. The fear of naked exposure falls within the orbit of shameful exposure, a fact which liberal thinkers traced back to dependency itself. But here there is a paradox.

Liberalism of the Lockean sort meant stripping away the fictions of honor—titles, privileges, rituals of rank. Montesquieu perhaps understood the consequences better than Locke. Defining who is then a virtuous, self-sufficing citizen means assessing a person's inner state of being; it means evaluating, as Mill said, how well a man can hold life together through coherent acts of reasoning. In probing this inner virtue, the Republic inevitably violates the line between public and private, "gets at" something deep in the character of the citizen; the language of personal independence is just that—deeply personal, a naked judgment.

Some framers of the pyramidal welfare institution therefore tried to work out its human side in a different way, since dependency of both a material and a social sort seemed to them a basic fact in modern society.

From its origins, though, the British founders of the modern welfare state knew they had a problem in treating clients as human beings in need yet respecting their autonomy. In 1939, John Maynard Keynes described the welfare state he sought to create in Britain as

> a system where we can act as an organized community for common purposes and to promote social and economic justice whilst respecting and protecting the individual—his freedom of choice, his faith, his mind and its expression, his enterprise and his property.[27]

The compound in Keynes's vision is the word "whilst": providing bureaucratic protection "whilst respecting . . . the individual . . . his freedom of choice . . . his enterprise."

Accounting procedures did not seem to this great economist to offer any solution. Nor did Mill's liberalism; consent to being governed still left the problem of how others governed the dependent. Rather, the welfare institutions he hoped to create would have to allow dependents to participate in the conditions of their own dependency; Keynes aspired to what might be called a democratic form of dependency. His intellectual probity lay in sharpening and making precise the institutional problem, without claiming an ultimate solution.

When Harold Macmillan wrote *The Middle Way* in 1938, he too was troubled by bureaucratic destruction of autonomy, a destruction he defined more globally. In the Soviet Union, he saw a bureaucracy which reached into the nether reaches of subjective life, by turns punitive and paternalistic in responding to what it discovered. In Western communism, the revolutionary vanguard seemed to reach inside the lives of the cadres, performing a character-reforming function akin to that of the bourgeois social worker. Was bureaucratic intrusion then bad in itself? Macmillan had only to look at Britain and America, where the state left people alone to starve, get sick, or go mad.[28]

The history of public housing offered a solution, of sorts, to the problem of coupling dependency with autonomy. Like charity workers before them, the fathers of the British welfare state wanted indeed to strengthen the independence of those they cared for, so their clients would be ready to be more self-reliant when economic conditions permitted. Mixed-income public housing provided one model. The historian Gordon Burke expresses it negatively, when he writes that nineteenth-century reformers feared that "slum-dwelling . . . away from the uplifting example of social superiors . . . might well lead to a pauperized and demoralized people who might cease to be industrious. . . ."[29] A more positive expression appeared in plans Ebenezer Howard made at the turn of the twentieth century for garden cities ringing the old British urban core; mixed housing, he thought, would provide the poor models for self-reliance in the behavior of their middle-class neighbors.

The logic underlying mixed-use housing resembles playing a musical phrase backward: policy has to address the psychological consequences of dependency first, the supposed erosion of self-assertion and self-esteem over the long term. This requires institutions which instill discipline, or provide role models and guidance strengthening the capacity for more independent action. This logic was meant to strengthen Howard's aspiring workers, just as it made a certain sense of the Peabody Trust's housing rules imposed on the poorest of the poor in the nineteenth century; rigidity begetting independence continues today, as the logic of military-style camps for juvenile offenders in America.

But there was no participation envisioned in this formula, no democratic dependence. Settlement-house workers like Jane Addams had long known that the poor must participate in the conditions of their own need. But her answer—the practice of personal reserve as an invitation to clients to become involved, could not help Keynes or W. H. Beveridge create stable, durable, comprehensive institutions.

The provision of autonomy within dependency was the great bureaucratic dilemma faced by the social-democratic creators of the welfare state. For their clients in hospitals, asylums, housing projects, or community centers, that problem translated into how one could escape becoming a passive recipient of care—passivity, not dependency, was the issue. Classic liberalism offered no solution, nor did modern critiques of total institutions.

Homeless adolescents are an extreme case of people who resist becoming spectators to their own needs. As homeless people, they need help which they cannot provide for themselves. As adolescents they are rebelling against authority and the controls imposed by adults; like all adolescents they are distrustful and cynical about the guidance they need. In flight from, rejected by, or abandoned by their families, they most urgently need structure to their lives in order to survive. What kind of institution could allow them then to participate in the conditions of their own dependency? How can they experience both support and autonomy?

It's a riddle I hardly know how to solve, but there does seem to me one important element left out. Autonomy, we have seen, is not simply an action; it requires also a relationship in which one party accepts that he or she cannot understand something about the other. The acceptance that one cannot understand things about another gives both standing and equality in the relationship. Autonomy supposes at once connection and strangeness, closeness and impersonality.

The history of welfare bureaucracy is one in which precisely this element of autonomy was excluded. It seemed to the welfare state founders that to provide for those in need required an institution to define *what* its clients need. It would have seemed irrational to provide resources without articulating their uses, but the result was that bureaucracy did not learn how to admit the autonomy of those it served. The homeless teenager was not treated as possessing a certain expertise about homelessness.

What impressed me about the cops in the squad car was that they indeed seemed to have learned from the homeless kids. Though they were hardly credulous or sentimental students, these two men thought they could only deal with these kids by giving them some mental credit. Back at police headquarters, at least in those days, the staff made use of information provided by the kids, but seldom of the interpretations they offered of how best to survive on the streets.

Big Brother explanations of rigid bureaucracy are not necessary to explain this blindness. As in the economy, so in welfare, the bureaucratic pyramid had come into being as a "search for order" within capitalist society; power drove the cartel, but lack of food, shelter, and health care drove the welfare state's search for order.

And as in the economy, so in welfare, the institutions of order had the power to reach deep inside dependent human beings, to touch their loyalties, their life narratives, and above all their sense of worth. The giant corporation did so to prevent strikes or to squeeze out productivity gains. Only the paranoid could believe that the welfare state *aimed*, similarly, at pacifying those whom it helped. But in practice these institutions, which sought to treat clients as whole human beings, made the great and glaring error of denying that the clients were competent to participate in the terms of their own dependency.

Chapter Seven

Liberated Welfare

When the young John Maynard Keynes resigned from the India Office in 1908, his superior wrote back sympathetically:

> I have never been quite able to satisfy myself that a government office . . . is the best thing for a young man of energy and right ambitions. It is a comfortable means of life and leads by fairly sure, if slow, stages to modern competence and old age provisions. But it is rarely exciting or strenuous and does not make sufficient call on the combative and self-assertive elements of human nature.[1]

From its inception, the rigid pyramid inhibited "the combative and self-assertive elements" in its most ambitious inmates. The bureaucratic frame originally put in place to foster "careers open to talent" had become ever less entrepreneurial as it included ever more people.

Keynes quit; others less ambitious had to be pushed, as security degenerated into complacency. The Indian writer Amit Chaudhuri well evokes that degeneration in describing an office given over to "a time-tested culture of tea-drinking, gossip, and procrastination. . . . It was, in a sense, a relaxing place to be in, like withdrawing to some outpost that was cut off from the larger movements of the world."[2]

A generation ago, large numbers of people leaped, or were pushed, outside the iron cage of welfare. The institutions which replaced rigid bureaucracy made fewer social demands on those who worked within; these same light institutions transformed the provision of care. Both those who leaped and those who were pushed found they had lost something in this transformed world, whatever its freedoms; they had lost a way to structure mutual respect.

The Disk

The repression of market competition inaugurated by Standard Oil had run its economic course by the last third of the twentieth century. "Globalization" is one way to name the forces which exhausted the old order—it is a catchall word, but bears in several ways on the social transformation of institutions.

An enormous pent-up demand around the world for products and services became apparent by the early 1980s. There was a great quantity of capital seeking targets of opportunity after the breakdown in 1973 of the Bretton Woods controls on money movements. Both supply and demand combined to spur corporations to adapt quickly to changes in market demand and money supply. Technological innovations via the computer made possible "global real time," the synchronization of communications and financial transactions around the world. Last, and perhaps most important, a change in power: stockholders began to reassert demands for short-term returns on investment, challenging management bureaucrats who had been content if things simply chugged along as they had before.[3]

What kind of organization could meet these demands? The change is exemplified in the manufacture of automobiles. Ford's managers dictated repetitive, routine labor, in offices as on the shop floor. Japanese auto manufacturers from the 1970s on defied the military logic of Fordism; they redesigned the productive process as teams of workers moving from task to task, product to product, as demand fluctuates and shifts focus; the new managers of Subaru insisted that laborers have no fixed niche in their plants. They invested capital in plants outside Japan; they monitored both demand and their own operations through a highly sophisticated computer-information system, tracking monthly, even weekly changes in markets. They made use of just-in-time delivery of parts to keep inventories low. Ford originally declared, "You can buy my car in any color, so long as it is black." The modern manufacturer employs "platform design" so that the same basic machine can be easily and quickly customized into many different versions of a car.[4]

Two institutional principles underlie such changes: the organization is flatter in form than the bureaucratic pyramid, and shorter in its time horizon.

"Flat" means removing the intermediate layers of bureaucracy in a pyramidal organization. IBM's organization chart shows a graphic instance of this radical surgery; in 1965 there were twenty-three standardized links in the chain of command, but by the year 2000 only seven degrees of formal separation stood between the bottom and the top. De-layering aims equally to curb sprawl at the base. Outsourcing and subcontracting is one way to shrink it. There's nothing new about outsourcing, which was practiced even in the heyday of the Ford Motor Works. What has changed is the sheer scale of this practice, a network of subcontractors and sub-subcontractors spreading throughout the world.

"Short" means replacing fixed functions by more temporary tasks in an organization. A Harvard Business School guru speaks of organizations in which "business concepts, product designs, competitor intelligence, capital equipment, and all kinds of knowledge have shorter credible life spans."[5] The new way of work emphasizes teams which come together to perform tasks and then split apart, employees forming new groups. For a flexible business to respond quickly to new market opportunities outside, however, these teams may well compete against one another, trying to respond effectively and quickly to goals set by the top. In the modern auto industry this may involve five teams working on five different versions of the same car. The result is to change the meaning of efficiency: there is an intentional duplication of effort, in order to stimulate innovation.

"Short" also refers to short-term return in the market, rather than long-term profit. In 1965, stocks were held by institutional investors on average forty-six months; in 2000, they were hold on average eight months. As a result, quarterly stock price has become far more important than in an earlier generation. Managers who can boost quarterly returns succeed; managers aiming for the long term have to defend themselves.

Weber and Michels evoked the power of bureaucrats in organizations bent on avoiding disorder. Today, shareholders and "stakeholders" are reasserting their powers over management; the owners of corporations want to be in control of its bureaucrats. Pension funds are now active participants in boardrooms; globalization has meant that shareholders around the world, strangers far from the seats of management, can sit in judgment of the organization. Corrupt or incompetent managers have always sought to hide incriminating data; what's new about a scandal like that of the Enron Corporation is both the number of outside "prying eyes" and the speed with which the corporate scam unfolded.

When businesses began to revolt against the architecture of the pyramid, they hit on the image of the "network" to describe this new flat and short construction, an organizational form loose and easy to recombine. Moreover, some management gurus have argued that the networked organization is democratic rather than militaristic, just because the network has fewer links in its chain of command. But this is a somewhat misleading claim; a "network" does not really convey how power works in such short, flat organizations. Instead, the two types of business architecture tend to different kinds of inequality.

Economists like Robert Frank have pointed to the income inequalities generated by modern corporations; there is a spread between the wealth accruing through bonuses, stock options, and salaries which sets off the corporate elite from the mass below. Frank calls these "winner-take-all" outcomes.[6] This increasing inequality is not just a product of managerial greed; it derives from the very way modern corporations function. This functional inequality results from the fact that modern work organizations operate somewhat like the innards of a disk player.

Within a CD machine, the central processing unit—a laser unit sending up a cone of light which reads the materials on the disk above—can scan various versions of a song on disk and select which it wants to play, or the order of materials. So too a flat, short bureaucracy contains a central processing unit. A small number of managers can rule, making decisions, setting tasks, judging results; the elements on disk can be reordered and reprogrammed quickly; the information revolution has given the central processing unit instantaneous readings on the total organization.

Flexibility thus permits a particular exercise of inequality. As in pyramidal corporations, the top can make sudden decisions about investment or business strategy without votes from below. Unlike in the pyramid, however, the execution of these decisions can be both swift and precise. In a pyramid, commands tend to modulate in content as they pass down the chain of command, altering a bit in each link. Conversely, when people at the top are dependent on thick layers of bureaucracy below, information changes as it passes upward; bad news often does not make it to the top.

Eliminate links in the chain of command and you can reduce this interpretative modulation. Instead, the surveillance and command powers at the top can be increased. Modern technology plays a crucial role here; thanks to computerization, top leadership can measure on a daily, even an hourly basis how well the troops are doing, markets behaving. Investors want transparent information rather than interpretations. True democracy is always slow—deliberative and unfolding. In a disk institution, slow becomes dysfunctional.

In place of minutely graded inequalities, then, the flexible organization permits a sharper distinction between elite and mass. Due to its effective command power is at the top, the flexible organization can function as a more "total institution" than the traditional bureaucratic pyramid.

During the boom of the last decades of the twentieth century, flat, short organizations proved better at seizing opportunities than the communities evoked by Amit Chaudhuri, in which people were oriented more to one another than to their work. Flat, short organizations made headway in global manufacturing and in financial services, the media, and computer software firms. The old-fashioned bureaucratic pyramid continues to function well for other kinds of businesses—those which have fairly stable sources of demand, or aim at long-term profit. The pyramid also has a strong hold on family-owned firms, or those which are not publicly traded.

As the boom of the 1990s ended, the experiment in flat, short organizations seemed in jeopardy. Firms in trouble needed stable relations with their suppliers, patient investors, and dedicated employees committed to getting businesses through hard times; the collapse of the Internet bubble aroused skepticism about the institutions of the "new economy." But flat, short institutions had entrenched themselves; no global business can be done without them, no new firm will ever be created on the principle of lifetime employment. More ominously, the flexible firm has become a model for welfare.

Disk Welfare

The sociologist Bob Jessop calls the application of new business models to the welfare state a "hollowing out" of its bureaucratic buildings by reducing the bureaucratic layers as well as the numbers of welfare workers and supervisors. "Hollowing out" the ranks of doctors, teachers, or social workers will not, of course, reduce the number of sick people, students, or the poor.

So reform of welfare bureaucracy has also required consumers of welfare to rethink the care they will receive: shorter in term and less fixed in content.

"Flat welfare," in the best reforms evident in some parts of the United States, shortens the links in bureaucracy while maintaining an adequate staff on the ground. Wisconsin and New York State are models in excising supervisory fat. In less-adept flat strategies, reformers have tried to follow the business practice of internal markets. This happened in the first flush of "reform" of the National Health Service in Britain, and in proposals current in both America and Europe to offer school-fee vouchers, so that parents can select among schools competing for their children.

These efforts to break up hierarchy are less adept because while the bottom line in business markets is price, in education or health, cost alone is no measure of quality. There is a further difficulty. It is particularly difficult for poor or poorly educated people to "shop" for schools because they can't refer to their own experience as a model of what they want for their children. All patients suffer a kindred difficulty in shopping for doctors or hospitals. Consumers of welfare need disinterested advice; in a market, no seller is disinterested. A cancer patient trying to choose a surgeon would hardly benefit from selecting the best salesman.

"Short," in welfare reform, means a state reducing its own responsibilities by limiting permanent or fixed guarantees, replacing these by more temporary acts of help. The most dramatic example of this in America and Western Europe is the cut in time people can receive unemployment benefits. Short welfare is indeed driven by practical need; in Italy, fixed retirement rules have brought the government's treasury to its knees, and fixed unemployment benefits in Germany and Sweden could pose the same threat. Like internal markers, short welfare which diminishes government responsibility shifts the management of fate back onto the individual.

As in flat, short corporations, the result is to create inequalities. The policy analyst Patrick Dunleavy has studied, for instance, the cleavage which reforms beget between passive dependents and more independent consumers of welfare.[7] The first are those requiring guidance; the second require only resources. Into the first category falls a ninety-year-old struggling to manage his or her pension investments, into the second that same person forty years before; into the first fall the perplexed immigrant couple trying to choose a school for their children in London, into the second fall the parents who have lived in London all their lives.

Dunleavy points to a tendency among reformers to offer a poorer quality of service to the passively dependent than to those who make decisions for themselves. Like Dunleavy, Jessop concludes that "reform" has meant a change from providing benefits "for all citizens as a right" toward a two-nations policy in which there is "a self-financed bonus for the privileged and stigmatizing, disciplinary charity for the disprivileged."[8] This result is somewhat akin to winner-take-all markets in the private sector.

Finally, as in work bureaucracy, so in welfare the flat, short structure can concentrate power. In welfare, the laser consists of centralized decision-makers determining who will be allocated resources: the American HMO, a private insurer, determines whether and how much doctors can treat patients. More broadly, in supposedly "devolved" systems of welfare, central government determines how much localities can spend, rather than what every citizen needs. Hollowing out a welfare bureaucracy reduces, as in business, the interpretative communication between layers which marks the bureaucratic pyramid. "Need" becomes an abstraction, a number, a datum instantly assessed from the top rather a negotiable human relationship.

Welfare-to-Work

In a business, demand greater than supply pushes up profits; in a welfare state, demand greater than supply produces misery. This is one compelling reason for diminishing welfare demand by putting welfare clients to work. Welfare-to-work is not an economic panacea; it does nothing to reduce health, education, or pension costs, which form the bulk of welfare state expenses. But money is only one reason to pursue this reform.

Work has long seemed character-building, increasing both self-esteem and respect from others. In the case of homeless adolescents, access to work has indeed provided profound emotional as well as material support, a strengthening of self-esteem shown in numerous studies. Adults on welfare who had the capacity to work but not the opportunities respond similarly well to these programs. However, welfare-to-work can create problems in families if pursued as an individual strategy, as when women go to work but their male partners remain unemployed.

Yet the work these new workers do complicates the issue of mutual esteem and respect from the larger society in a different way. The work available to former welfare clients is usually low-skill service labor in flexible businesses: work in fast-food restaurants, or as contract-term guards, or as temporary hospital aides. The flow of welfare clients into the bottom of the flat, short organization is not, it should be said, invariable; some parts of American government experimenting with welfare-to-work have put time and cash into training the newly working poor for viable, skilled jobs with a future, and unions have taken in some former welfare dependents in the same caring way. The larger social issue which confronts most new workers lies in the organizations they are entering—organizations whose ways of working are, for the middle class as well as for the poor, not very cohesive.

In pyramids, people who loyally served the institution were meant to be rewarded for their loyalty. Now seniority, service, and loyalty have fewer claims on firms. In an appropriately titled book, *Only the Paranoid Survive,* the president of the Intel Corporation declares:

> Fear of competition, fear of bankruptcy, fear of being wrong, and fear of losing can all be powerful motivators. How do we cultivate fear of losing in our employees? We can only do that if we feel it ourselves.[9]

Detachment makes sense in such organizations; a consultant who managed a recent IBM job shrinkage declares that once employees "understand [they can't depend on the corporation] they're marketable."[10] People are meant to treat work as an episodic activity, a series of tasks as one jumps from place to place.

Flat, short forms of work tend to forge weak bonds of fraternity among workers. The social analyst Robert Putnam has found, for instance, that coworkers account for fewer than 10 percent of American friendships; when people are asked to whom they would turn to discuss an important issue, fewer than half listed a single coworker.[11] Weak fraternity is a logical social consequence of those jobs in particular in which workers spend a short amount of time together, as in teams rotated every six or eight months; people simply do not get to know one another.

Moreover, the flexible work world tends to breed passivity in its bottom echelons. In an unstable institution, where people have no viable claims on the organization, they tend to keep their heads down in order to survive; the sociologist Charles Hecksher has found even survivors of downsizings and reengineerings do so, hoping to become invisible to the managerial tigers, fearing the next blow of the corporate ax.[12] The sociologist Jill Andresky Fraser calls this "emotional detachment as a survival strategy."[13]

These social deficits of flat, short organizations apply particularly to new, needy workers at the bottom. Without outside intervention, new workers have trouble forming support networks in such workplaces; the climate of detachment, institutional distrust, and passivity is not good for learning how to work. Their problems are sharpened because the last and lowest hired are often the first fired; without expensive employment assistance, these entry-level jobs can prove particularly demoralizing to workers who formerly relied on welfare.

The problems faced by those in welfare-to-work point to a basic fact about all flexible organizations: their social bonds are weak. Observers of this work world such as Jeremy Rifkin and Robert Howard have argued that work stress hardly makes for a real social bond; nor does the pleasantness, seeming cooperativeness, and curb on raw aggressiveness cultivated under the name of "social skills" at work. There may be affability, but without much commitment; the "voices" at work described by Albert Hirschmann, articulate because committed, have fallen silent.[14]

Rifkin, Howard, and many other critics of labor have therefore concluded that community life will have to make up for the social deficits of flat, short organizations: community serving as a compensation for work. What sort of remedy is it?

The Remedy of Community

In my childhood, the remedy of community would have seemed obvious. After the war, when troops came home and the factories producing military supplies shut down in Chicago, men in Cabrini faced the problem of where to find work— unlike their wives, who were usually employable as household servants. The men congregated at the southwest corner of the project each morning, waiting for contract-labor bosses who would pick them up in trucks to do casual day labor in the city. Most men hated this flexible labor, in which they were nothing more than a temporary pair of hands. That hatred only reinforced their attachment to Cabrini, the highly regulated home in which they became men again, not hired hands.

Classical sociology makes a contrast between *Gesellschaft* and *Gemeinschaft*—the first naming merely function, the second more emotionally full relations between people. The contrast is fleshed by contrasting the behavior of strangers and neighbors, in big places versus small ones, behavior which emphasizes rules versus behavior more spontaneous in character. Just as the

Cabrini workers preferred *Gemeinschaft,* so do many modern welfare reformers; it seems a less demeaning context of care.

But this simple contrast is not quite cogent, for successful welfare "in the community" often has to operate by impersonal and rigid rules. Consider, for example, some instances of how good streetworkers in communities actually succeed with the most difficult cases: juvenile criminals.

One of the most effective youth organizations in Chicago, the Chicago Area Project, began in the 1930s as an effort to reduce juvenile delinquency. For several generations it did street work with delinquents, work which required sharply honed skills. Adolescent criminals frequently try to "wind up" social workers, for instance, by being as sullen or aggressive as possible, trying to provoke the adults into loosing control; responding emotionally would spell disaster. Moreover, the adults who learned how to cope with this on the streets were not locals, but outsiders who had drawn over the years on the accumulated knowledge of others.

The time required to make programs like this work is not that of casual, daily life. A contemporary program for young drug addicts in Paris, located in the streets around bus stations in the city, supposes about eighteen months are required to establish an effective network of contacts with the community of drug addicts, and then about five years to wean them individually off drugs.

In Chicago as in Paris, good street work requires a planned narrative whose denouement is exit from crime, if not addiction; the Chicago Area Project looks highly bureaucratic to an outsider only because this long exit requires the assistance of doctors, legal advice, and financial support for the offenders themselves and occasionally for their families. On the street, to assume help which eschews formal bureaucracy means providing little help.[15] Serious care means moving beyond the timeframe of flexibility.

In looking to more spontaneous and voluntary forms of communal welfare, however, we are expressing a desire in ourselves for experiences of community. And that desire has a quite specific locus. Its origins lie in a particular religious past; the desire for community has taken on a peculiar cast, over the course of time, by intersecting with a particular experience of religion.

In traditional Judaism and Islam, welfare in the community required individuals to execute obligations to others in obedience to divine law. By the Middle Ages, Judaic commentaries on the Old Testament became quite concrete about the amount of charity families must give each year (roughly 10 percent of household wealth) and what should be given to whom—for example, what specifically needed to be provided to orphans of one's first cousins. The Koran was similarly concrete; Islam's institution of the charitable *wacq* appears in medieval Koranic commentaries as an extended family aiding individual families. Catholicism also formulated compassion as duty; the papal encyclical *Rerum Novarum* of 1871 focused on the obligations of the church itself to those oppressed by the modern economy.

Protestantism, however, emphasized the spontaneous, voluntary character of providing help to others. Luther wrote that charity cannot be commanded; for Calvin, compassion is a "free gift of self."[16] Wordsworth's poem "The Old Cumberland

Beggar" attacks the Catholic (and Judeo-Islamic) belief in compassion as duty:

> . . . who of the moral law
> Established in the land where they abide
> Are strict observers.

> In this cold abstinence from evil deeds,
> And these inevitable charities,
> Wherewith to satisfy the human soul?[17]

In the 1540s, Archbishop Cranmer sought to reform communication in churches by commanding that a minister speak "with a loud voice, so turning his body [toward the congregation rather than addressing the Cross] that the people might hear."[18] Whereas in the Catholic confessional box people do not speak face to face seeing each other though they may be only inches apart, Protestant group speaking meant to involve the eye as well as the voice—the whole human being engaged. And so to reveal the whole human being; nothing is meant to be hidden from others in the community.

Face to face, it should be said, does not necessarily imply intimacy. In the cafés and coffeehouses of eighteenth-century Paris and London, for instance, strangers felt free to speak face to face. You entered, sat down at any table, took a coffee, and talked, whether you knew the others at table or not. You spoke using a theatrical language and gestures which would hardly have been appropriate at home. The somewhat artificial character of coffeehouse speech permitted strangers come to the city from the provinces or from other countries to share a common language, and so to exchange information, to find out what was happening—it was for this reason that insurance companies like Lloyd's of London began as coffeehouses—but not to know one another better as individuals.

Puritans would have made bad companions in a coffeehouse. Protestantism pushed face-to-face communication in the direction of intimate revelation—to reveal oneself, and to experience the revelations of others, became a kind of final test of mutual respect. By the 1830s Tocqueville noted how far this revelatory intimacy had advanced: what the American volunteer gets from good works is a personal relationship; in Tocqueville's view, charity had become a means to the end of creating small, local communities.

The danger here was and remains mistaking charity for friendship—a confusion which attended both British and American poor-visiting in the nineteenth century; the bourgeois "Friends" often sought to form face-to-face relations with the poor they visited. More modern forms of American volunteerism have been similarly personal, as in the "Big Brother" organizations which provide role models and surrogates for missing fathers.

The danger of confusing help and friendship is, as work with juvenile criminals makes clear, a structural one. Very few friendships could or should bear the weight of providing sustained or effective help. Just as a refusal to respond to provocation or manipulation is an impersonal, professional skill, so the long-term, intensive commitment of time to a client cannot follow the deepening of intimacy in a friendship; the caseworker hopes eventually the client will be able to loosen the bond.

The characteristic figure of American welfare since Tocqueville's time has been the local volunteer, and the social history of volunteering has turned largely around the ways volunteers themselves had to discover and deal with the confusions of help and friendship. The importance of sorting out what it means to volunteer has grown, in recent years, as the "reform" of big, pyramidal institutions has progressed: ever more burdens are thrown on the volunteer's shoulders. Making the idea of community service seem even more important, however, is the superficiality and instability of social relations in much of the modern work world.

How effetive, then, is volulnteer care?

"Who Is My Stranger?"

Today, the American volunteer has become a fairly well-defined social figure. As elderly people live longer and in better health, they have the time, and their willingness to volunteer has indeed grown. Equally encouraging, students and young people increasingly do public service projects as part of their education. But individuals in the thirty-to-fifty age group, particularly those in their thirties, donated their time significantly less in 1998 than in, say, 1975.[19]

This gap in the middle is sometimes explained by the increasing pressures of work, since the working hours of middle-aged Americans have lengthened considerably in the last generation. But that explanation will not alone suffice. Judged in terms of their involvement in other civic activities as quick as writing to newspapers, middle-aged Americans are less engaged; in Britain, the proportion of young voters who vote, or watch political news, is steadily falling.[20] The Islamic and Jewish fathers were wise, perhaps, in separating community from personal desire.

When he coined the term "individualism" in the second volume of *Democracy in America,* Tocqueville drew out this problem in the most dramatic way. Individualism, he argued, consists in love of family and friends, but indifference to any social relations beyond that intimate sphere. Equality only makes the problem of individualism worse: because most people seem the same as oneself in tastes, beliefs, and needs, it seems one can and should leave it to others to deal with their own problems.

Voluntary organizations are an institutional counterweight to individual, egalitarian indifference to others. Today, the raw amount of wealth the United States puts into nonprofit charities and foundations is staggering, about twelve times the rate of contributions in Britain. American tax laws have encouraged this accumulation of charitable wealth, exempting nearly tax dollar for dollar contributions made to the nonprofit sector. Continental European nations have also accumulated a large financial base for nonprofit, civil-society activities; their sources include pension-fund charities and government donations to "parallel civic organizations," as well as purely personal donations.

However, while in both America and Europe the raw amounts given to the not-for-profit sector are growing, the amounts contributed per individual are falling; it is the wealthy few who are swelling the coffers. At the end of the great economic boom of the 1990s, Americans donated less per head than they did in 1940, at the end of the Great Depression.

So the individual impulse to give remains an issue; those individuals most likely to give are people who then volunteer for community service. In the United States, Robert Wuthnow has found that most "institutional kindness" comes from volunteers who want to transform something in their own characters, adding to themselves and their experiences of others what they cannot find in the cold world of functional or rational relationships.[21] Sherryl Kleinman and Gary Fine have shown how voluntary organizations attract recruits by promising, indeed demanding, changes in their "core selves."[22]

The political analyst Robert Putnam has sought to probe this appeal by drawing a distinction between what he calls "bonding" and "bridging" social relationships. Bonding relationships consist of those associations which are "inward-looking and tend to reinforce exclusive identities and homogeneous groups." This is the realm of face to face; it continues to be strong. Bridging relationships are "outward-looking and encompass people across diverse social cleavages." This is the civic realm of strangers, and it is growing ever weaker.[23]

The difference comes into focus in considering a particular voluntary activity like donation of bodily fluids. In all Western societies, blood donations rise dramatically during times of war or national attack; people spontaneously "bridge." Under more tranquil circumstances, Americans do not—at least, their rates of voluntary, unpaid American blood donations have declined during the last decade, whereas in Britain they have held up.[24] Within a ten-year period beginning in 1987, American blood donations fell from eighty units a year to sixty-two units.[25]

The British sociologist Richard Titmuss sought to understand what numbers like this reveal about civil society. *The Gift Relationship,* first appearing in 1970, established a sliding scale of donors, from what he called Type A, "the donor who sells his blood for what the market will bear," to Type H, the altruistic donor who most closely approximates "in social reality the abstract concept of a 'free human gift.'"[26] American donors spanned the spectrum from A to H; British donors were more clustered at the free-gift end. More than 70 percent came from families in which no one had been a blood recipient.

To explain the motives for the free gift of blood, Titmuss—a no-nonsense researcher—had to pose an abstract question: "Who is my stranger?" He meant to signal the most important fact about Type H motivation: these freely giving donors had no idea where or to whom their blood would go. Just as they were not returning blood their families had used, there could be no face-to-face interaction with recipients. In his view, community is strong when that interaction is not needed, weak when the gift is personalized.[27]

A report by Gillian Weaver and Susan Williams on British donations of breast milk, following Titmuss's work, reports a similar framing of the impersonal gift among donors. Because breast milk—given mostly to prematurely born infants—is hard to express and requires repeated sessions to accumulate in usable amounts, its donation is far more arduous than gifts of blood. Again the rate of donation is higher in Britain than America, and again in Britain the rule of donation is "the knowledge amongst donors that their donations are for unnamed strangers without distinction of age, sex, medical conditions, income, class, religion, or ethnic group."[28]

None of these figures should be taken as evidence that Americans are selfish: they point, rather, to a structural problem in the American communal model. On the positive side, this model encourages personally fulfilling activities such as mentoring; on the negative side it creates an impediment to perceiving and taking seriously the needs of strangers. It could be said the dilemma is peculiarly American, a compensation for lack of a viable, more impersonal public realm. But the context is larger. The spread of flexible institutions of work is more than an American phenomenon; so is the effort to restructure welfare along new bureaucratic lines. Both arouse the desire for a compensating, countervailing community.

Volunteering is a poor remedy for binding strangers together, or dealing with social complexities. It lacks what might be called an architecture of sympathy—that is, a progressive movement up from identifying with individuals one knows to individuals one doesn't know. The prerequisite of autonomy is missing too: the willingness to remain strangers to one another in a social relationship. If the possibilities of making personal contact and sharing understanding diminish, the impulse to engage weakens. The Dutch sociologist Abram de Swann has argued that the civilizing functions of the welfare state require the "generalization of inter-dependence" in society.[29] Yet the sphere of mutual regard is too small, too intimate, when the volunteer is taken to be the ideal figure providing care to others. Saying this is not to denigrate volunteers, but rather to criticize the idealization of these "friends" when something other than friendship is required.

Usefulness

In the same measure that welfare reformers have celebrated the local volunteers, they have attacked public service workers—and indeed the very ethos of public service.

For the last quarter century, more largely, the honor of public service work has been slighted. What's striking is how those subject to this onslaught have defended their self-respect.

They've done so by asserting the value of useful rather than flexible labor.

A recent report on two hundred public service workers in Britain (in which I participated) shows, for instance, how they've kept their sense of usefulness intact. A London street sweeper declared to one investigator:

> On Mondays I certainly get job satisfaction. It's the worst day for rubbish because there's only a skeleton staff on at weekends. When I look back at the street I've just done and all the piles of rubbish are gone and it's clean, I'm pleased.

A dog handler for the customs services who sniffs out drugs with her pooch says, "I feel valued both by my employer and the public. People know it is a worthwhile job, stopping drugs coming into the country." A fitness instructor for a local government declares war on fat; he believes keeping people fat-free is a political project.

It was particularly surprising to find that many believe they are better at their jobs than people in the private sector. The fitness instructor, for instance, believes he can spend the time needed, and get deeper into the problems of fat, than if he were a salesman of exercise turning over clients as rapidly as possible. So, we found, do many nurses in the public health service believe they do a better job than those working for private hospitals. At the other end of the social scale, the managing director of a public service fund has been offered three times his salary to work in the private sector, but has resisted because he believes the jobs are less challenging.

The defense mounted by these public service workers

focuses not just on one's value *to* the organization, nor just on one's value to the general public, but on the act of doing something useful. Usefulness takes on the characteristics of craftwork, characteristics which include an egoistic involvement in the task itself. There is no reserved holding back about the value of this work to others, but neither is there *amour-propre* in Rousseau's sense of invidious competition—simply a belief the work is worth doing.

American public service workers share these values, but in those professions particularly aimed at caring for the poor, American social workers tend to stay in public service for much shorter lengths of time than their British counterparts; rates of turnover in American social work jobs have steadily increased in the last generation. The increasingly flat and short practices of health care are driving doctors in both countries out of public health services. In America, the teaching profession has divided; tenured teachers remain in their jobs longer than in Britain—or, surprisingly, than in Germany—while there is in all three countries an enormous Sargasso Sea of floating part-time teachers who move in and out of the profession.

Service to others certainly matters to public service workers, but the craft aspect of usefulness helps people to persevere under conditions in which their honor is frequently impugned. The work itself provides objective standards of feeling oneself worthwhile. The street sweeper likes a clean street, the handler of drug-sniffing dogs likes handling dogs.

Focusing on the craft of useful work separates this kind of caregiving from compassion. It does not turn on pity for those in need. The craft dimensions of useful work serve as a caution against the error of believing that doing good necessarily entails self-sacrifice. Usefulness must, by contrast, have an inherent value, a focus on a specific object, which gives the service worker satisfaction.

In 1708, Joseph Addison's *Spectator* printed a popular ditty which ran

> God bless the squire and his relations,
> And keep us in our proper stations.[30]

It was the traditional idea of a community, one in which everyone knows their place. Addison was ambivalent about the "honour of station," and his modern readers are even more so. Pyramidal bureaucracies could provide everyone a place and a proper function, see them as whole human beings, but at the cost of denying them participation.

The institutional innovations of our time embodied in disk bureaucracy do not place people stably, and do not see people whole. In compensation, people may seek to connect to others, voluntarily, locally, face to face. A social void may indeed be filled this way. But there is no solution to the problem of welfare here. The welfare client in need, but treated with scant respect, cannot be liberated simply by opening the iron cage, no more than the modern worker has been set free by unlocking the iron cage. It is not liberation from formal constraint but a better connection to others which the welfare client requires.

Depressing as the problems of welfare are to most of us, they are satisfying challenges to many public service workers. When dedicated to their jobs, these workers have tried to maintain self-respect by doing something useful; those they serve are strangers.

There is self-interest in this impulse to do something useful, and also an acceptance of social distance. Perhaps these elements suggest something about how self-respect and recognition of others might more largely operate, in an unequal society nothing like the stable world evoked by Addison.

Part Four

Character
and
Social Structure

Respect is an expressive performance. That is, treating others with respect doesn't just happen, even with the best will in the world; to convey respect means finding the words and gestures which make it felt and convincing. Just as Fischer-Dieskau performs respect for his pianist Gerald Moore, so does, I think, the professional youth worker who learns how to criticize homeless adolescents without turning them off.

Throughout the last century, anthropologists sought to understand the rituals which affirm mutual respect, in societies quite different from our own. These ritual performances helped legitimate inequalities of status and wealth, and were disturbing for just that reason to many of the Westerners who studied them: status and hierarchy can feel so *natural* to the celebrants of a rite. So anthropologists sought to discover also other ritual performances which diminished inequalities and bound members of a tribe more closely together—as though "primitive" society also contained clues for the Left in the West.

Both art and anthropology are useful guides in exploring how people in our own society might express respect so as to reach across the boundaries of inequality. In looking for those clues, we might discover something of not just social value. These expressive acts, when they occur, reveal something about how character takes form: character as that aspect of self capable of moving others.

Chapter Eight

The Mutual in Mutual Respect

Qui touisiours prent et rien ne donne
L'amour de l'amy abandonne.

(Who nothing gives and always takes
His friend's love forsakes.)

—*Sixteenth-century French proverb*[1]

In the 1760s, following an old custom, the aunt of the diplomat Talleyrand threw open the doors of her best drawing room once a month to the servants and peasants who lived on her estates.[2] She sat in a chair, they stood in a semicircle around her; on a table before her were a vast number of small bottles, each with a label written out in her own hand. A laborer or servant would come forward and describe some illness or ache for which he or she needed a remedy; the aunt would select one of the bottles, which contained medicines made from herbs grown on the estate; she would then explain how to take the medicine and offer words of encouragement. The "patient" would bow, accept the bottle, withdraw back to the semicircle, and the next person would come forward. This was the "pharmacy" of the duchess.

The surprise of her pharmacy lay in the fact that Talleyrand's aunt was quite deaf. The servants acknowledged this fact by studiously not referring to it, describing their ailments in low tones; she too behaved as though she heard perfectly, and so thoughtfully judged which bottle would be best.

The participants in the pharmacy were performing a ritual. Directions for performing are lodged in shared memories of what people should do to play their parts, perform their roles; they know where to stand, what to do, what not to say. This ritual demands that the performers play their parts well. The rhythm of the ritual requires that no one speak out of turn, or describe a complaint for which the peasant knows the duchess lacks the appropriate bottle. She herself observes a discipline in her starring role: she does not simply furnish the bottle a peasant "needs," but knows she has to say something about how to use it; she thereby makes a little verbal gesture of communication. But this communication is binding just because it is a performance—a fiction if you like—since she cannot hear and yet they speak, showing her their moving lips.

Talleyrand himself, not noted for sociological interests, would no doubt have found it pedantic to view this ritual as one in which inequality and mutual respect coexist. Yet the inherited places and hierarchy of a traditional country estate could be legitimated if all felt they had an honorable place—which the ceremony helped them to feel. A thousand variations of the scene in her drawing room oiled the machinery of traditional society.

In one way, this ritual is not alien; since there's little we can do about our friends' illnesses, amorous disasters, or financial missteps, the advice we often give them resembles the duchess handing out bottles of herbs. Something of the same play of deference and inclusion occurs in any good discussion; the listener judges when not to interrupt, the speaker when to solicit a question. In its shared fictions and knowing silences, the fitions of the pharmacy found a modern equivalent among those friends of the Boston Brahmin who treated her selling job as a lark rather than a necessity.

Still, the ratification of inequality offends modern sensibilities. The source of that offense seems located in the performing bond itself. The duchess and her peasants are bound together just because they act well with each other. To understand just what kind of social bond performing makes, it might be useful to compare this "pharmacy" to a less politically charged performance—say a performance of the Brahms Clarinet Quintet in B Minor, Op. 115, a work Brahms completed in 1891.[3]

An amateur group can hack its way through the notes but will usually make a mushy soup out of the sound. The challenge Brahms sets his players is how the thick texture of the score can be clarified. Brahms's expressive markings give some but not sufficient indications of how to go about this; the players have to figure the problem out for themselves. They do so by inventing rituals for performing together.

For instance, playing in unison—sounding different notes on different instruments at the same time—is a basic form of rhythmic cooperation, but it is harder to cooperate this way than the listener might imagine. Brahms throws a particularly tough problem of rhythmic unison at his players at the opening of the quintet. For the first twenty-four bars we have traded back and forth a fluid group of melodic bits. Suddenly, at bar 25, the fluid movement stops when all five instruments are called upon to play three loud, crisp chords in unison. The middle chord is the hardest, because the shortest; a sixteenth note snapped out.

In rehearsal, the performers have to work out how to emphasize the fact that the music suddenly stops what has come before. One solution is to starve even the middle, briefest chord of its full duration. The clarinetist may have the toughest time physically achieving this, but all the players must feel that short time together, in order to make the break felt. The bond between performers begins here, in using eye contact and body gestures to signal to each other.

Or take the problem of balancing dominant and subordinate voices. Brahms sets this problem in the quintet with a signature rhythmic device; this is a syncopation which ties for one instrument a sixteenth note to a longer note across the bar, while another instrument sounds only on the bar. Off-beat syncopation occurs in a particularly dense passage in the first movement at bars 58–59 for the viola and second violin, while all hell is breaking loose in the other instruments, on the beat.

Here collaboration demands self-restraint, which the inner voices achieve by another little expressive gesture: they don't swell on their syncopation. In theory, holding oneself back keeps one at a distance from others. In performing the quintet, avoiding the danger of swelling out instead achieves distinction and articulation within a whole. By holding back we make our presence felt—which is reserve's most subtle and more positive side.

As in all expressive labor, there is an objective problem to be solved: the soup of notes. The performers together will have to solve that problem by learning to play as one, in unison, but also by learning how to hold back or how to dominate. The gestures in sound they create become rituals which orient them to one another and speak together.

Rituals in social life are equally complicated acts of knitting people together—with the great difference that the "social text" is not a written musical score; it emerges through trial and error, and then becomes engraved in memory as tradition. The hold of tradition comes from this knowing already how to express oneself to others; whereas for chamber musicians, performing traditions can help, but the real social glue occurs when the performers have to work things out for themselves.

Rituals of equality and fraternity in the early phases of the French Revolution tried simply to substitute equality for inequality as their legitimate subject. In the "Festival of the Unity and Indivisibility of the Republic," held in Paris on August 10, 1793, the revolutionaries constructed a giant naked goddess, from whose two nipples there gushed a stream of milk-colored water which was to be drunk freely and equally by all citizens.[4] But these rituals of equality soon withered. Their conventions did not command conviction.

There's another illuminating contrast between performing Brahms's quintet and participating in the ritual of the pharmacy. One musical group's performing gestures are not invalidated by a different, indeed contrary, interpretation by another group of players; the spell of convention is secure when we are playing well. A servant or peasant incensed by this ritual of inequality will try to break the spell of convention, however, most brutally by showing the old woman he or she knows she is deaf.

Breaking down ritual's power, its binding spell, was indeed how modern society has sought to root out the hold of inequality over people's sense of themselves: treat inequality as a blunt fact, not as a performance. In the view of sociologists such as Peter Berger, society pays a price when it tries to do so; it weakens the very meaning of social honor. Berger explains this price as follows:

> In a world of honor, the individual discovers his true identity in his roles, and to turn away from the roles is to turn away from himself. . . . [Today] the individual can only discover his true identity by emancipating himself from his socially imposed roles—the latter are only masks, entangling him in illusion. . . .[5]

The individual must "emancipate" himself or herself from roles, play-acting, from collective fictions; this emancipation culminates in rejecting bonds of social honor.

The elaborate festivals conducted by the Nazis instantly make the point of how destructive the ritual bond can be. But from that experience many anthropologists contest the possibility of scraping away the power of ritual—so fundamental a collaborative act in human relations. About rituals of inequality, one school of anthropology has therefore sought to turn the tables, redefining inequality itself, drawing on research in non-

Western places, to show a different performing bond from that which appeared in the drawing room of the duchess: a bond first rigorously described in 1922 in Bronislaw Malinowski's classic *Argonauts of the Western Pacific*.[6]

Performing Inequality: The Socialist Way

Malinowski's subjects were people living in the Trobriand Islands, off the coast of Papua New Guinea. They were bound together by giving and receiving gifts. They did so at market festivals at which craftsmen carved necklaces and bracelets which constituted the wealth of the Trobriand Islands and were, and still are, distributed. These ceremonies required arduous travel in special boats between the Trobriand Islands; hence Malinowski's title, which compared these tribes to the heroic voyages of Jason and his fellow Argonauts in ancient Greek mythology.

Capitalist markets emphasize getting something. The Trobriand peoples emphasize giving something away. The donor assumes an air of modesty, falsely apologizing that this bracelet or necklace is all that remains of his own possessions, casting it at the feet of the receiver. The person to whom the precious object is given must play his part, behaving as if he cannot accept it, acknowledging the real power of the gift by snatching up the bracelet or necklace just for a moment before dropping it again, as if afraid of it.[7]

In tone, the Trobriand festivals evoke Japanese *tanomu* behavior signaling dependence; both make a point of personal insufficiency. The self-effacing behavior has its Western echo in the conduct of that idealized gentleman who does not boast and is diffident about his possessions. What makes the rituals challenging to us, mutual to its participants, is that there are no losers.

A man or group who "succeeds" in giving away shell jewelry obligates others; they will in some future time have to return the shells, reversing the ceremony. In the meantime, however, each party remains bound to the other for mutual assistance. This bond is not that of largesse, the present of gold which debases the receiver. As Trobriand rituals passed down from generation to generation, the diverse groups in the scattered Trobriand Islands knitted together through a rhythm of giving, receiving, assisting, and returning. Such exchange makes "enemies into friends," in the words of the anthropologist Annette Weiner.[8]

Malinowski's discoveries in the Pacific appeared to many of his Western readers to hold a mirror up to their own society, particularly to the possessive individualism and greed of Western capitalism. As far back as the emergence of market society in medieval cities, the historian Georges Duby has argued, "the profit motive steadily undermined the spirit of largesse [as simple generosity]." Karl Polanyi, in *The Great Transformation,* sees the social balance between giving and profiting shift most decisively at the end of the eighteenth century. Gareth Stedman Jones concentrates on the "deformation of the gift" in London of the 1860s. "Whatever the date," the historian Natalie Zemon Davis observes of this line of argument, "the direction of change is always the same."[9] Which is an ever more possessive, less giving economy, diminishing in turn the spirit of mutuality.

Malinowski's mirror reflected a more positive possibility to his colleague Marcel Mauss, who was also Emile Durkheim's nephew. From his uncle, Mauss had first learned the precept that reciprocal exchange knits people together in groups; Malinowski refined the precept by indicating how objects like shell jewelry become symbols of mutual respect in a ritual. Now Mauss added a liberating ingredient.

He believed that the Trobrianders held up the example of a ritual of inequality radically different from those which knit together the *ancien régime*. In the Trobriand Islands, people's resources were unequal; more, their exchanges were asymmetrical. By giving, an imbalance was created between individuals and groups. Mauss argued that just the imbalance created an expressive bond between them—and that there is a lesson for socialism in that asymmetry.

What he is after is evident the moment we think about what happens in an ordinary capitalist exchange: I sell you caviar and you pay me in money, gloves, or porcupine quills of an equivalent value. The two sides balance, the market clears. But this is not, Mauss says, an exchange which binds us emotionally. Our relations will take root only when we stop reckoning equivalence. To take another prosaic instance, in a restaurant when the bill comes, someone begins calculating what each person ate and how much he or she drank in order to arrive at his or her fair share of the bill; the conviviality of the evening is aborted. We instead act as friends to others when we contribute without such reckonings, perhaps covering without fuss someone at table who is poor.

Mauss had a large end in view when he began to develop the principle of asymmetric exchange: the "social" in socialism. In the last years of his life, Mauss tried to make anthropological sense of Marx's phrase "From each according to his abilities, to each according to his needs." The Trobriander debt suggested to him that this relationship never clears; there is never an equivalence. As an anthropologist, he believed rituals like those of the Trobrianders could represent and articulate that imbalance so that people were connected by performing a rite together, rather than estranged by the inequality.

His writings on this score are more probes than finished ideas. But he had gotten far enough to understand that he might have discovered a basic principle about the proper conduct of a welfare state. That large end was first announced at the conclusion of his book *The Gift,* published the year of his death, 1950. Mauss says the welfare state owes the individual something other than a simple monetary return on contributions. Why does it?

> The worker has given his life and his labor . . . to the collectivity and . . . to his employers. . . . *Those who have benefited from his services have not discharged their debt to him through the payment of wages.* The state itself, representing the community, owes him, as do his employers, together with some assistance from himself, a certain security in life, against unemployment, sickness, old age, and death.[10]

A lifetime of hard work has no monetary equivalent; therefore a welfare system should not be based on the money people have paid into it. Workers should contribute to their own pensions but not be cut off when the contributions run out: the market in old people should not clear. The asymmetry between work and welfare is the foundation of Mauss's brand of socialism.

He observed that many traditional societies practiced asymmetric welfare; he disputed that modern society is too poor to afford it.

And yet *The Gift* is perhaps a misnamed book, for Mauss believed that those who benefit must give something back, even if they do not and cannot give back an equivalent. They must do so to achieve respect in the eyes of others and their own. The anthropologist Mary Douglas applied this same precept to compassion. "Charity is meant to be a free gift," she writes, "a voluntary, unrequited surrender of resources." The difficulty is that "though we laud charity as a Christian virtue we know that it wounds."[11] If we ask nothing in return, we do not acknowledge the mutual relationship between ourselves and the person to whom we give. "There are no free gifts," Douglas writes.[12] Put simply, reciprocity is the foundation of mutual respect.

It may seem that this precept excludes the blood or breast milk donor who does not know the recipient, or the volunteer who just sends a check to an organization; they appear to be making a free gift. But there is, however, a transaction involved, if impersonal or defined in the head of the donor: he or she is giving something *back* to society. The public service worker doing a useful job will make that same transaction mentally. Though an accountant may never be able to tally what a blood donor "owes" society, still the donor will invent the debt, and make the gift.

Here is an imagination of responsibility which cannot be confirmed materially. Mauss's student Alain Caillé says all symbols acquire an emotional power just because we can't translate them into equivalent values. Concretely, this is what happens when a judge invokes "The majesty of the law" and the court falls silent, the felon bows his head. "Majesty" has a compelling effect, but one which is hard to explain in other words. In daily life, Caillé says, we are constantly giving and receiving meanings without being able to measure them.[13]

Mauss tried to reimagine malign inequality as an absence of return. Exchange binds people by some kind of return, symbolic or material, but exchange need not, in its asymmetric form, equalize resources. Practically, Mauss wants the welfare state to leap over differences of class and wealth in returning care to them. Mauss wanted to break the capitalist ethos of giving back to people just, and only, what they "deserve."

What role does ritual play in this socialist redefinition of inequality? Another of Mauss's heirs, Pierre Bourdieu, tried to answer this in his researches among the Kabyle peoples living in the hills of Algeria.[14] He recounts, for instance, a village man who had come down in the world and in falling had become a thief, one day stealing the stones of a neighbor's retaining wall. The victim declares, "It's not by such means that a lawful and just house is built." The person addressed is the brother of the thief. The victim in the village will not have this: "You are wrong not to accept responsibility with your brother in front of me."

Just at this moment the magic of ritual and its bonding power begins. Neither the victim nor the other tribesmen want the stones back; they want the brother to talk. He frankly discusses the thief's corruption but also invokes their father's virility in producing many sons, and the tribe is now satisfied. The brother has exchanged words.

When ritual binds people together, Bourdieu more largely

observed, it does so by allowing them to "mutate" material fact into some expressive gesture which can be shared—and sustained. An economic exchange is a short transaction; the new institutional forms of capitalism are particularly short-term. By contrast, a ritual exchange, particularly of this asymmetric sort, creates a more prolonged relationship; reciprocal speech acts become like threads woven into cloth. The welfare state Mauss imagined in France, like the rituals Bourdieu studied in the hills of North Africa, have the character of social projects which cannot be finished, which remain ongoing just because they are ambiguous. They are like stories which can't conclude, in which there is no denouement—whereas in the world of transactions, in truly flexible capitalism, sharp, rapid endings rule.

Peter Berger's observation about the binding power of rituals could be rephrased: why doesn't modern capitalism generate them? It would certainly be in the interest of the powerful if something akin to the pharmacy of the duchess existed in work or in the welfare state. The reason this hasn't happened is both capitalism's insistence on the symmetry of exchange and its increasingly short framework of shared time.

Of course, blaming capitalism risks becoming an exercise in ideology. There were few binding rituals in Cabrini because we had little to give back—certainly no money. Had we been allowed to participate in the running of the housing project, we would at least have given back our participation, our time—a return which would accord with Mauss's principle of asymmetry. But even this return would have been gratuitous. The welfare administrators *didn't need us*. They didn't need us to finance, to design, or to govern the housing project. That same problem exists in the most elemental form of inequality, the inequality of talents. The rocket scientist can perfectly well proceed with his or her calculations, whether or not the average person understands—a source of the craftsman's or technician's indifference to others.

Still, the Maussian view of exchange is compelling, as compelling in the arts as it is in society. It certainly reveals the relations in which performing musicians stand to one another. Even the sound experience which seems least Maussian—balance—is in fact a confluence which doesn't compute. In the Brahms quintet, the clarinet has throughout its range a penetrating power matched physically only by the G string of the cello when sounded close to the bridge; the adjustments all the players have to make to that penetrating power require displacements of bow and reed pressure.

Mutual cannot mean equal, either in art or social ritual, if equal in turn means equally distributed. The bond of performing, the experience of mutuality, refuses that accounting. But what is missing in the Maussian account of ritual is the character of those who interact. In music the character of a performer—if we follow Dietrich Fischer-Dieskau—lies in sound rather than self, and for music this precept may suffice. In society, it cannot.

Self-Respect and Mutual Respect

In a study of a black ghetto in Philadelphia, the ethnographer Elijah Anderson came across a young man he calls simply "Robert," a dealer in drugs arrested at seventeen for violently assaulting another drug dealer.[15] In jail, Robert begins to change. The codes of the street which earned him respect from other kids as well as cash come to seem hollow; he begins teaching himself to read—particularly the Koran, other religious works, and books about the history of race in America. Robert resolves to lead a decent life in tune with his own conscience when he gets out.

Anderson charts just how difficult it is for Robert once the young man returns to the streets of Philadelphia. The ex-criminal finds three other young people similarly determined to make a new start; together they find an elderly man willing to set them up in a street business, selling fruit and hot dogs. At first Robert forfeits the respect he had from his gang buddies for going straight, and at the same time he has also to fight against the outside world which threatens his venture.

The most remarkable part of his story, revealed by Anderson's own remarkable powers as an interviewer, is how Robert must learn to recast the ghetto rituals of toughness and manhood to survive in the neighborhood. He uses street smarts—from turns of phrase to threatening physical gestures—in order to make a turf for himself which is "clean"; eventually he earns a respected place in the community for this toughness, now put to decent uses.

But Robert is not now dependent on others for his self-respect. The "code of the street," as Anderson calls it, the mutual exchanges which generate black brotherhood, are rituals which Robert has learned to manipulate, and also to step away from. Indeed, he has become inventive in manipulating the street rituals he uses, knowing when to threaten, how to appear suddenly to give in; rather than being a puppet of the code of the street, he has become a puppeteer.

Truly mutual exchange has ended and, in its place, the governor of his relations to others is his own self-respect, founded on conscience. This may seem to be the liberal story of individualism, brought home to the black ghetto, the kind of story imaged by the philosopher Adam Seligman in describing how "conscience comes to replace honor" in modern society: "the focus of moral agency is relocated to the individual and separated from the externalities of role and status."[16] But Robert could not survive without carefully eliciting the respect of others.

The difference of his life on the streets from liberal theory cuts further. The values of right and wrong he learned in prison from the Koran are neither his own nor subject to negotiation on the street; he would perish emotionally as well as materially once he started to cut corners with these rigid precepts. The anthropologist Frank Stewart fears a kind of amorphous, individual relativism when codes of group honor break down:

> The honor code is reduced to something like the maxim "to thine own self be true." . . . One can say that almost any set of values that one holds dear counts as one's honor code, and that one's title to honor is the possession of a proper sense of honor.[17]

"Any set of values" will not do for Robert. To keep himself going, every exchange on the street must be morally symmetric; though he's willing to give hungry people credit, he also judges them according to an implacable standard of right and wrong.

Finally, Robert has in one way made a simple, free gift to others. He has not left the community. People who pull themselves together much more often flee the scenes where their lives came apart—this was true of many kids who escaped

Cabrini in the generation after mine—and there's no shame in doing so; the "code of the street" could so easily drag them down. Fearing that pull, he nonetheless returned, and stayed, to prove something to himself.

The story of this exceptionally strong young man brings out a conundrum in less tested lives, a tension between self-respect and mutual respect. Exchange binds him to others on the street, but not in ways anthropologists like Mauss envisioned. Moral dictates of self-respect outside the process of exchange anchor him; just because Robert feels the power of that inner rule so strongly, he can give himself back to the community.

Robert's life on the street points to the element missing in Mauss's account: A person who holds fast to a set of beliefs despite conflicts with those around him has to think them more important than the values which bind groups together. Here it is inequalities of value which matter, and it is just such inequalities which give shape to character and social structure. On the street, that assertion of character translates into a problem of self-protection. This problem arises because of the street's very power of ritual performances of respect in concert with others, those body gestures, words, and acts which compose the "code of the street." The players are both brothers and threats to self-respect.

Reflecting on Robert's story led me to appreciate more the social bond of performing music. There are certainly conflicting interpretations and conflicting egos in musical performance; there are wrong shared gestures, collective expressions which fail—but self-protection is largely alien to playing chamber music. Yet Robert's story is evocative precisely because of the difficulty of protecting oneself while connecting to others.

. . .

In sum, ritual exchanges build mutual respect—whether in the Trobriand Islands, in French country châteaux, among musicians, or on the streets of an urban ghetto. So deep is this power of expressive exchange that it can be turned to the most contrary ends: inequality can feel good, or nonpossessiveness can seem natural. The art of expressing respect, like any expressive act, does not imply justice, truth, or goodness. And as Robert's experience on the streets of Philadelphia makes clear, expressing mutual respect can do an individual harm.

Still, I don't believe mutual respect is merely a tool to grease the gears of society. This art has consequences for the people who practice it; exchange turns people outward—a stance which is necessary for the development of character.

Chapter Nine

A Character Turned Outward

The Secure Actor

The old-fashioned English phrase "a solid character" invokes someone who could justly think of himself or herself with respect. The American version is someone who feels secure in himself or herself, the French "comfortable in one's skin." All these usages suppose self-confidence.

As I found when as a young man my hand failed, self-confidence can prove an ambiguous foundation for self-respect. At the polar extreme from my rarefied existence, a street kid like Robert found he could maintain his self-respect only by an uncertain turning outward, taking in and testing new values.

The anthropologist Claude Levi-Strauss took the matter one step further. He believed self-confident individuals could do themselves a profound injury; they could become paralyzed by feeling comfortable in their skins. The question he poses is how those who do turn outward can still retain a core sense of themselves.

In doing the fieldwork for his most famous book, *Tristes Tropiques,* Levi-Strauss in the 1930s came upon a tribe in the Brazilian rain forest who seemed paralyzed by self-confidence. The Bororo Indians at first impressed him by their skill and their fierce pride in making villages. These villages, they said, directly reflected the cosmos. By observing the heavens at night, the Bororo deduced that the universe was circular in shape, divided within into four pie-shaped pieces. The ancient Romans saw the night sky in the same way, and the Bororo, like the Romans, applied this celestial harmony to the ground; the Bororo village took shape as a circle of huts, the perimeter inhabited by women, the center of the circle containing a men's house. Four different kin groups occupied the four slices of ground within the circle.

The design oriented all the tribe's daily activities. Women worked outside the circle; men and women made love in specific quadrants, depending on their family background; the men hung out only in the center; the village prayed in a space between the perimeter and the center, in one quadrant only. "Codes of the street" became here codes of the wedge, the periphery, the center, and then of the circle as a whole; mutual respect meant doing the right thing in the right place.

During his wanderings in the areas near these villages, Levi-Strauss discovered that the fixity of Bororo planning made the tribe vulnerable. The Bororo had attracted the attention of the Silesian Fathers, a missionary group seeking to convert them to Christianity. These priests did not argue cosmology with the natives, since the Bororo found the Christian story of Genesis a bit primitive: a messy Garden provided to overgrown children forbidden to sort matters out for themselves. The Silesian Fathers sought instead to break the hold of the Bororo worldview by a simple change in the village plan: Levi-Strauss observed that "the surest way [to conversion] was to make the Bororo abandon their village in favor of one with the houses set out in parallel rows."[1]

Abetted by various natural disasters, the priests forced the Bororo out of their traditional village, to profound effect. Disoriented, the Bororo lost confidence in themselves; Levi-Strauss says that "once they had been deprived of their bearings and were without the plan which acted as a confirmation of their native lore, the Indians soon lost any feeling for tradition."[2] But the tribe was not simply a victim of the outside world. Because the Bororo communal edifice was so tightly constructed, the survival of the community was fragile; change in one part brought the whole structure down. Their very coherence invited victimization.

To the Bororo, Levi-Strauss contrasted forest migrants who were just then, in the 1930s, beginning to move to Brazilian cities—a great diasporic wave which seemed to Levi-Strauss emblematic of what would happen to village and farming people around the world in the twentieth century. The anthropologist observed that many of these Brazilian migrants were not similarly paralyzed. They kept up pride in traditions, yet could adapt these to new circumstances; the old religions survived transit to the world of automobiles and Coke. They indeed wreaked a certain vengeance upon the missionaries, who frequently blanched at masses in which Mary appeared in the shape of a forest orchid or the infant Jesus as a sacred monkey.

Why did these migrants avoid the fate of the Bororo? Levi-Strauss doubted that "modernization" acted like a beacon beckoning Indians to forget who they once were. Instead these Brazilian migrants to cities seemed to him to resemble émigrés hiding icons in their suitcases as they fled revolutionary Russia for Paris; the Brazilian migrants packed their mental bags with fixed pictures from their villages of what the world should be like and the ritual practices which affirmed that picture; unlike the Bororo, they did not demand consistency and coherence in their worldview.

The anthropologist called *bricolage* the process of disassembling a culture into pieces and then packing it for travel. Levi-Strauss called *métics* those who practiced *bricolage,* transforming an ancient Greek usage for outsiders into the idea of people who can remember where they came from even while accepting they can no longer live there; this kind of travel he called *métissage,* a journey in which there is change but not forgetting. The traveler thereby retained a certain measure of security and self-confidence in facing, and accepting, the incoherence of the outside and the new.

Tristes Tropiques, like Malinowski's *Argonauts of the Western Pacific,* became a parable for many Western readers: how to preserve a sense of self and group in the process of change. The secure *métic* packed more cultural baggage than he or she needed, knowing some of the pieces in the suitcase would prove useless. Still, the abundance was reassuring, allowing some give and take. Whereas the Bororo were rigid; their problem seemed to embody the paralysis closer to home facing traditional groups like the Boston Brahmins, groups which would wither if their identities remained too secure.

There are elements lacking in Levi-Strauss's account. He does not explain why people might indeed seek something new. Missing also in this account is how the human being interprets the alien and the new.

Restructuring Security

There is a structure to this interpretative act. The structure is well illustrated by performing music; specifically in playing the piano, and even more specifically in using the wrist.

A dot written over single notes or chords in piano music indicates a pointed sound, an attack. The pianist is often first trained to execute a dot by holding still the knuckle of the hand and flexing the hand at the wrist; this wrist flip then becomes ingrained as a habit. Whenever the young pianist sees a dotted note, he or she will draw on this habit, without thinking about what to do. But wrist work can't remain in this fixed groove.

In the course of Beethoven's piano sonatas, for instance, the dot mark comes to stand for ever more varied attack sounds, some like drumbeats, others like triangles, still others like cymbals.[3] The full variety of Beethoven's dots appears in the third movement of Sonata No. 30 in E Major, Op. 109; in the second variation of this movement, the dotted notes can be executed by wrist flips, but for the dots marked in variation six the old habit for performing dots will not serve: variation six jolts the pianist into conscious awareness that the flipping wrist action of variation two now will inhibit fluid speed. So the player has to stop and ponder, to experiment; the score gives no instructions to the hand about what to do.

Temporary confusion and surrender of control are not the end of the story. Pianists may discover the solution I found, that of holding the wrist firm and making the knuckles do the work.[4] Once this knuckle-flip movement has been consciously worked out, the practice returns to the realm of habit; the player is no longer self-conscious about making the motion. But the most important effect of this newly acquired knowledge is on the other physical gestures of the wrist; they loosen up and interact with the new motion, knuckle and wrist becoming ever more coordinated in the whole hand.

This learning curve has a formal name: it embodies a passage from tacit knowledge to explicit knowledge and then back to tacit knowledge. The tacit realm is formed by habits which, when once learned, become unself-conscious; the explicit realm emerges when habit encounters resistance and challenge, and so requires conscious deliberation. The return to the tacit realm is not to the knowledge with which one started; if now unself-conscious, new habits have enriched and modified the old.

Some followers of Hegel believe this is what he meant by "dialectics," a thesis, its antithesis, and then a synthesis, though the parallel is not quite accurate in that Hegel believed the end result would be a heightened self-consciousness. In music, self-consciousness is the enemy of art; the expanded repertoire of gestures has to seem just to happen, without calculation—which is what we mean when we say of a pianist that he or she plays "naturally."

Movement from the tacit to the explicit differs from Levi-Strauss's account of *métissage* in two ways. First, the contents of one's habits and beliefs are transformed in meaning when they encounter resistance or unfamiliar demands. It is as though, unpacking in a foreign country, the migrant discovers the precious possessions he has packed have changed.

Second, self-confidence has changed its character. Self-confidence was rooted in the initial stage of tacit knowledge; what made it work, before it was challenged, was its seeming naturalness. These were not people doubting at every moment about what to do, what to think. An enlarged repertoire of expressive gestures, of social practices, has to recover that functional confidence. Levi-Strauss acknowledges the need to construct naturalness, but thinks this can be done only if people feel their core values and behaviors haven't changed.

There are practical reasons why the tacit realm has to encourage the confidence of acting naturally, rather than self-consciously. First of all because this permits efficient communication between people. To take a very modern instance, consider how a Web page is constructed. The following example is the programming instructions which establish the Web page for the writing team of John Seely Brown and Paul Duguid:

```
<HTML>
<HEAD>
<TITLE>John Seely Brown</TITLE>
<META NAME="GENERATOR" CONTENT=
    "MOZILLA/3.01Gold
(X11; 1; SunOS 4.1.4m)[Netscape]">
</HEAD>
<BODY TEXT="#000000" BGCOLOR="#FFFFFF"
LINK="#0000FF" VLINK="#52188C"
ALINK="#FF0000">
<CENTER><TABLE CELLSPACING= 2
    CELLPADDING=10
WIDTH="550" HEIGHT="60">
<CENTER><P>!--<td width=550 align=center
valign=middle><img src="images/wip2-banner.gif"> </td>-->
```

And so forth for another dozen lines.[5]

To see all this explicitly on the screen would make communicating with the pair extremely difficult. "Efficient communication," the subjects of this Web page observe, "relies not on how much can be said, but on how much can be left unsaid—and even unread—in the background."[6] That background is the tacit context; the practical foreground is recognition of a name.

The philosopher Michael Polanyi says of the tacit realm in general that "we know more than we can tell."[7] Similarly, the literary theorist M. M. Bakhtin asserts "the primacy of context over text," so that every time we read a sentence we nest its value into many other sentences of which we need not be immediately aware.[8]

If efficient, the tacit realm also provides emotional support, in the form which the philosopher Maurice Merleau-Ponty calls "ontological security."[9] To worry in a love affair constantly about "the meaning of our relationship" would kill it. Similarly, trust requires tacit understandings; unremitting, questioning consciousness carries a poisonous anxiety. "Ontological security" is more than a psychological experience; the bureaucratic pyramids of work and welfare also sought to provide it.

Most of all, the realm of tacit understandings, supporting assumptions, ontological security, provides the background which permits a person to focus on doing a particular task well. The Bororo were, Levi-Strauss remarked, proud of their collective skills as village makers. And justly so; designs of their work I've been able to find show an enormous sophistication in projecting the flat cosmological image they saw in the sky onto hilly ground—whereas the Romans tended to simplify this work by grading the ground flat.[10] The Bororo made villages somewhat the way we make Web pages; the background instructions from the heavens, taken for granted, permitted them to focus on the practical "foreground" difficulty of molding the earth. If the Bororo had to question why the heavens are as they are, their labors with ax and saw would have been less confident.

Yet in that "ontological security" lay their eventual doom. Another, more prosaic, musical example may give a clue to why this would happen. In the so-called Suzuki method for teaching stringed instruments, little bands of tape are applied to the strings on the violin or cello a young child is using; the tape exactly tells the child where to place his or her fingers to play in tune. Security is provided, but the beginner is not empowered. Once the little bands of tape are removed, the child often is at sea; he or she has not been listening before to the exact sound of the string, and so suddenly plays badly out of tune.

The shrinking of reality for the sake of ontological security is one reason why Freud drew his famous comparison between the human mind and the city of Rome:

> Now let us . . . suppose that Rome is not a human habitation but a psychical entity with a similarly long and copious past— an entity, that is to say, in which nothing that has once come into existence will have passed away and all the earlier phases of development continue to exist alongside the latest one. . . .[11]

At first, the comparison seems just to convey how tacit knowledge is lodged in the psyche; Freud's point is, however, to empower the mental archaeologist, the person digging down into the ground. Conscious excavation is necessary for the sake of survival in a hostile world, where little can be taken for granted—just as in the Suzuki method the young violinist is not empowered by security, nor is the village craftsman. Freud differs from Bakhtin or Merleau-Ponty in believing tacit knowledge induces a *false* sense of security; if feelings of security are indeed necessary to form a self, they will not sustain it in time.

Tacit knowledge provides, then, a picture of the world we take for granted, and doing so we can communicate effectively, focus on executing specific tasks, trust others, and feel confidence in ourselves. When Burke evoked the virtues of tradition, in his attacks on the French Revolution, the traditions he defended were of the tacit sort, the bonds between people they take for granted, bonds which, just because unspoken, just because habit so long practiced, were stronger than any "idea" of community. But to believe tacit understandings will endure is to succumb to a false sense of security.

The Turn Outward

The modern institutional realm, with its ever-changing, short transactions, wants to rescue people from that false sense of security. This new institutional regime puts a particular emphasis on breaking the bonds of ingrained, unconscious habits, even if these have served perfectly well in the past. The institution uses information technology to eliminate the often tacit mutual understandings which modulate information as it passes layers in the traditional bureaucratic pyramid. The new order seems instead to require explicit, self-questioning knowledge.

This credo is in a way but the modern reflection of the proposition put to Burke in 1792 by English advocates of the French Revolution: trust in things as they have been must always break down. While obviously true, this truism is not simple. From some breakdowns, some ruptures, people learn nothing; from others, they turn themselves outward.

In the 1930s the philosopher John Dewey found himself trying to make sense of what painters learn when they challenge themselves. Thanks to the collector Alfred Barnes, Dewey had access to a set of pictures by Matisse, Picasso, and Braque—then unfamiliar figures in America. In the collection there is a photograph of Matisse staring with visible distaste at one of his own canvases, an early masterpiece; we don't know exactly the reason for the painter's frown, though we do know at this time in his career Matisse feared going stale by repeating himself. The act of self-criticism is a subject Dewey took up, as a result of his exposure to the Barnes collection, in the book *Art as Experience*.

This book is in large part a study of the moment when tacit knowledge is challenged to become explicit. Like Merleau-Ponty, Dewey believed in the orienting, initial need for tacit knowledge; "Only when an organism shares in the ordered relations of its environment," he writes, "does it secure the stability essential to living."[12] But he wanted to understand why an artist might voluntarily surrender control over that expressive stability. His answer was both simple and not simple: simple as the desire to learn something new about the world, not simple in that, Dewey said, a person has to take responsibility for the breaking down of his or her own tacit understandings. He called that taking of responsibility, embodied in Matisse's frown, a "surrender."

We understand a little better this word by tracing its provenance. In the *Essay Concerning Human Understanding*, Locke wrote, "Self is that conscious thinking thing . . . which is sensible or conscious of pleasure and pain, capable of happiness or misery. . . ."[13] Whereas in "The Treatise of Human Nature" Hume asserts that "when I enter most intimately into what I call *myself*, I always stumble on some particular perception or other, of heat or cold, light or shade, love or hatred, pain or pleasure."[14] For Locke the self is "that conscious thinking thing" which disciplines sensation; reason is master in the house. For Hume the key word is "stumble"—by accident, by force of circumstance, unbidden sensations flood us. The self then becomes animated in treating the stumble as an opportunity rather than a threat to self-control. Dewey took the side of Hume rather than Locke, but took Hume one step further: "I have to trip myself up."

Dewey stood godfather to a school of psychology which sought to understand in ordinary life what happens when people surrender rather than simply loose control. These psychologists, notably Anna Freud, view that act of temporary surrender as a "renunciation of possession"; by suddenly letting go, a person is restimulated—as we might imagine with Matisse, the master who feared becoming stale.[15] The commonsense way of expressing this activity is as a self-testing. Again, the expression is simple and not simple: simple in confronting the resistance, not simple in staging the test. The phrase "renunciation of possession" seeks to convey letting go of a habit, consciously exploring something new and difficult, but actively so, not as a person defeated by the outside world. In declaring that "form follows failure," the computer technologist Henry Petroski tried to convey something akin; the good programmer tries to make programs malfunction, not wait passively for things to go wrong.[16] Conscious learning occurs only when a person is actively involved in pursuing difficulties, staging them.

The appearance of self-conscious, explicit understanding differs from the cultural changes which Levi-Strauss called *bricolage*. He imagined consciousness as an awareness of how to situate customs and habits in new circumstances. If successful in this task, the *métic* continues to accept on faith what he or she believed before the journey began.

But that was not the experience, for instance, of Renaissance Venetian Jews when they were first forced into isolated ghettoes in the years 1511–15. Most of these Jews were strangers to Venice, many having fled the persecutions of the Inquisition in Spain after 1492, others being traders from the Levant who lodged in the city during the first decade of the sixteenth century. Segregation of these foreigners in the islands of the ghetto forced Jews to practice communal reading of the Bible and Talmud at night, when they were shut in; to stay awake, Jews became avid coffee drinkers.

For a generation, no one thought about the habit of drinking coffee; the most profound experience open to the ordinary Jew, reading Talmud, stayed intact—a symbolic *métissage* of the sort Levi-Strauss envisioned, this migration of the Word to the night. In a second generation, though, that change came under scrutiny: was this artificial stimulus to religion a good thing? The Talmud makes no mention of coffee, but the Venetian Jews argued about what the Talmud would have said, if only the Fathers of the Word had known its taste. The second generation was making difficulties, the older generation said, when none need be; survival in the closed ghettoes was hard enough. But to the young the historic message of the Talmud had taken on a renewed life, "the Word in Diaspora" incorporating in its meanings the new conditions of enforced nightly segregation.[17]

Such a narrative rhythm shaped the cultural migration of Muslims and Christians as well as of Jews. Levi-Strauss has riposted that in these journeys the sacred texts themselves were not rewritten, indeed could not be revised; only commentaries, addressing fragments of the whole, could be added. But this reply fails to take into account the power of the Word, whether in Jewish or Islamic form, as a living presence in the lives of believers, a presence in their lives only because they feel present, themselves, in the sacred text.

The act of turning outward I have taken to embody a condition of character as well as of understanding, a new relation to other people as well as to shared symbols like those contained in a religion. For this turn to occur, something has to happen deep within the individual. "Turning outward" means the prisoner reforms rather than is reformed; he cannot simply be prescribed another, better set of social practices.

But it would be naive, indeed folly, to believe that society encourages this change. It is particularly a folly to accept on faith the professions of belief in "change from within" on the part of modern organizations. In the "disk" form of bureaucracy that I discussed in a preceding chapter, the reality of change is that it is imposed from above; in disk businesses, employees do not vote on mergers and acquisitions; in welfare disks, the unemployed do not vote on the length of their own benefits. What makes disk organizations distinctive is the ideological effort to present these controls as representing the subject's own desire for change. The reality is an inequality of power; the ideology is a shared desire for innovation, initiative, growth. Disks speak John Dewey's language but they hardly practice the "renunciation of possession."

This gap between language and practice explains a pattern now appearing in fieldwork and ethnographies about new institutions. Subjected to change, people do not feel themselves changing. They do not become more self-conscious in ways that open them up to others. The psychologist Daniel Kahneman believes that for the mass of modern workers, risk-taking inspires depression and foreboding rather than hope; people focus more on what they have to lose than to gain; they are being gambled with rather than themselves gambling.[18] What Albert Hirschmann calls a mentality of "exit" rather than of "voice" results.

What disk organizations make clear is that the turn outward in society, if not in art, requires financial resources, or a thick network of professional contacts, or control over others. At the top, change and risk can thus be managed without a person coming apart. But lower down in the modern institution, risk can be depressing just because these powers are lacking.

To say turning outward is a character strength may suppose a person is also strong in society—stronger, indeed, than others. Inequality reappears. Yet risk is not the only measure of the turn outward. Risk is, after all, self-interested; a person wants to gain; the new things he or she discovers are but a means to that end. Turning outward can also be simpler, and less self-interested—a matter of curiousity.

The nineteenth-century essayist William Hazlitt wrote that "the human mind is . . . naturally interested in the welfare of others."[19] Hazlitt chose his words carefully; he did not assert people are inherently generous, only that they tend to be curious about their neighbors. What makes us so? Were we certain about how the world works, Hazlitt argued, we would not take much interest in social affairs; only when "normal life" ceases to seem normal are we engaged. But there is no necessity forcing us to do so; we could get on, indifferent to others as we have been. This "natural interest" can come only from within, from our own curiosity, not from circumstance alone.

Levi-Strauss saw the dangers of lacking curiosity in the doomed history of the Bororo, but *métissage* is no answer for this lack. It emphasizes how the past can be preserved rather than how the present can be engaged and explored. Artistic practice furnishes a real model for turning outward, as in responding to the challenge posed by a strange dot in music. But inequality and power over other people are not at stake in that response. Social practices of the sort now celebrated by disk institutions furnish a restrictive model for this character strength: risk is celebrated, rather than disinterested curiosity.

What most complicates the shaping of character—if a person does turn outward, changing his or her ideas and sentiments through the influence of new people or events—is return to the world he or she has left behind.

The Difficulty of Return

Changes in behavior or attitude usually happen long before people become aware they have changed. It took a third generation of Venetian Jews for the religion of the night to become a practice generally accepted and naturalized; it took Robert several years before he could manipulate the code of the street in new keys, knowing what he was doing. It takes even longer for those who have not made a journey to understand those who have.

This difficulty seems obvious, yet bears on a large and complicated subject: group identity. Untested tacit social knowledge is like a group portrait, a shared image of how things should be. Tested social knowledge takes the form of a narrative, a shared story of change. The Bororo before the advent of the Silesian Fathers shared an image of their place in the world; the third generation of Venetian Jews shared a history. The sharing of a common image is both equal and instant; the sharing of a history is more arduous. Individual life histories entwine in complicated ways over time, and the insights which history has vouchsafed to one person it may have withheld from another.

Images classify: who belongs in the group portrait, who does not. The old American laws that assumed a drop of black blood made one black are an extreme of such classification, a tinted skin imposing a total identity. A shared history can also rigidly classify, as in the sharing of national narratives separating the "true" Serb from the person whose family happens to have lived in Serbia for several hundred years. Yet the personal act of narrating one's history to another person can also break down such rigidities. The narrator wanders from his or her point, the listener interjects something obscurely relevant; wandering off point often prods a sudden, conscious understanding for both. In this uncertainty of narration lies one key principle of mutual respect.

The group photograph provides a certainty of content: we are Muslims, Jews, blacks instantly recognizable to one another; we respect each other because we know who we are. Whereas all that mutual respect requires of listeners to a narrative is that they listen—like soldiers in a trench at night recounting to one another the histories of their families; all this mutual bond requires is that each sense others are paying attention in the dark. The content matters less. The difficulty of returning lies just here. Like the old buddies of Robert, the listeners may attend to the story of a transforming journey yet cling, still, to their own fixed picture of the world.

The German word *Weltanschauung* roughly translates as "outlook on the world," shared by a group: it also implies something clear to be seen. The anthropologist Gehlen said that people have a fear of the unfinished character of human life; a collective worldview relieves that fear of insufficiency by providing a simplified image into which the individual is at last integrated. This was the guiding principle Gehlen perceived in the rigid, definitive urban designs for Nazi Berlin made by Albert Speer. A more humane version was Max Weber's, for whom a *Weltanschauung* comes into being in order to answer the question "Why does suffering exist?" Society must provide an answer, and then stick to it. According to both, the picture of "us" dominates, overshadowing any story in which differences and discontinuities emerge.

The person who returns to others with disturbing news has, somehow, to impress on them that his story bears on their lives. But for the reasons given by Gehlen and Weber, it will be hard for him to express himself this way. For instance, Levi-Strauss's contemporary Erich Auerbach had escaped the Nazis by going into exile in Turkey. Deprived of books, unable to speak Turkish, Auerbach meditated on the problem of exile. There was a lot in his German past, he decided, he had taken too much for granted; he should have seen earlier what was coming. In exile, he knew, he would perish as a victim, dwelling on the shattered fragments of his life. In *Mimesis* he declares that in modern society "the tempo of change demands a perpetual and extremely difficult disposition toward inner adaptation and concomitant crises."[20] Just because the longing for stability is a recipe for disaster, a person will survive only by becoming "conscious that the social base upon which he lives . . . is perpetually changing through convulsions of the most various kinds."[21]

Yet in returning to the West after the war, Auerbach felt even more a stranger than when he left. The trials he experienced in exile elicited sympathy from his listeners, but prompted no reflection on their own condition. Germans clung to the image of themselves as victims, Americans to their manifest destiny to do good for others. His own turn outward, the profound reexamination in Turkey of what it meant to be European, seemed consigned to the pigeonhole of a private history. Perhaps, he concluded, Gehlen was right: pictures of identity are necessary, sustaining group illusions, even though these pictures, these tacit understandings, are bound to betray those who believe in them.

In an ideal world, groups would change through drawing on just those transformations of individual character which exemplified curiosity, an unexpected pleasure, or the lessons of unforeseen suffering. Distant as is this ideal, still a narrator can inspire respect in recounting his story. This expressive performance is the only hope we have of breaking the power of collective group images, of tacit knowledge which paralyzes our sense of society and of ourselves.

In a way my own story is done. I've charted a necessarily complicated relationship between society and character which might, just might, lead people to treat each other with mutual respect. For this to occur, people would have to practice exchanges of a peculiar kind; they would have to break down in certain ways their own tacit assumptions and shared pictures of the world. And yet my story is not done, because these elements of character and social structure came to vivid and indeed violent life in the politics of my youth, and indeed in the politics of my own family. So I have to conclude where I began, with fragments of my own biography.

Chapter Ten

The Politics
of Respect

The Old Politics

In the 1970s the Russian poet Joseph Brodsky arrived in New York after being expelled from the Soviet Union. In his homeland Brodsky had committed lyric poetry and other crimes; in New York he quickly settled in. Books and papers littered his basement apartment in Greenwich Village, the telephone rang constantly, but very little cooking was done in this nest. Thus I often gave him supper at my house; deprived of meat in the Soviet Union, he insisted on great slabs of American steak, chatting about friends and daily life between bites. My own family, however, eventually cast a shadow over these cozy evenings.

In the mid-1980s, Brodsky noticed on my bookshelf a new, large, blue-bound volume called *Communist Functionary and Corporate Executive,* by William Sennett. This was the autobiography of my uncle, based on an oral history compiled by researchers at the University of California.[1] Since my parents had parted almost as soon as I was born, I knew about this uncle mostly by hearsay. He had been something of a glamorous mystery to my mother's side of the family; rumor perhaps inflated his revolutionary exploits, but the mystery was that once having quit the Communist Party, he soon became a wealthy capitalist.

The Blue Book confirmed at least the exploits. My uncle lived to act. His autobiography recounts how he joined the Communist Party in 1931, then went with my father to fight in the Spanish Civil War. William Sennett's early life was filled with strikes, violent demonstrations, and run-ins with the police. After the Second World War, he served the Party as labor organizer, undercover agent, and publisher until 1956. In that year Khrushchev had viciously repressed a revolt in Hungary, shortly after denouncing Stalin's totalitarian crimes. By 1958 my uncle finally had had enough and quit the Party. Within a few years, he was managing a transportation company; within a decade, he was a powerful boss.

How and why this occurred was not really explained by the autobiography. His account of becoming rich is laconic and flat in tone—as though for a quarter of a century my uncle watched someone with the same name climb the capitalist ladder. Nor did he turn his back on the past. "I am a Socialist," my uncle affirmed, and this "has nothing to do with acquiring personal wealth." The evil of twentieth-century communism was its lack of democracy, my uncle had finally decided, but the poison of totalitarian rule could be purged, and something would still remain. As an elderly man Sennett could still declare, "I am no longer a Communist with a capital C. But I am, in essence, a

communist with a small c, believing in the concept and the ideology of communism."[2]

I lent the Blue Book to Brodsky, wondering if any of this
would make sense to him. At first it did. To Joseph, Sennett's
unfolding story seemed a pilgrimage of youthful faith, com-
pounded by American innocence, eventually giving way to
adult disillusion—the standard narrative of Western radicals
with a conscience. But Joseph's neck muscles tightened when he
read aloud the concluding passage I have quoted above.
Snapping the Blue Book shut, Joseph declared, "Comrade
Sennett has learned nothing."

In the arrests and persecutions which hounded Brodsky
from 1959 to 1964 (punishments included a forced stay in
Moscow's Kashchenko Psychiatric Hospital and exile under
pain of hard labor to the Arctic village of Norinskaya), his per-
secutors accused him repeatedly of "parasitism" (*tuneyadstvo*)
and of being a "misfit" (the word in Russian, *izgoy*, evokes a
person who doesn't know how to behave).[3] These formal
charges indict social crimes, rather than political offenses like
running an underground radio.

For Brodsky the evil of totalitarian socialism was its tight-
laced social bond. Brodsky's friend Czeslaw Milosz has pointed
to the state's limits to hold captive inner life; still, there was
intense pressure on people to conform in public, even if they
reserved conscience in private—as when one of Brodsky's pros-
ecutors took him aside to say "I'm sorry" before destroying the
poet in court. Slavery to the social was the issue: that's what my
uncle, in Joseph's view, had failed to learn.

This charge struck home. I had only to think of my father
and various members of my mother's family; they also had left

the Communist Party, in the 1930s, more in horror of its claustrophobic embrace than because they ceased to be radicals in spirit. But the Blue Book also surprised me. Rather than being the self-serving apologia of a Party hack, my uncle's autobiography revealed that he made a bad Communist from the start.

In 1934, for instance, the Communist Party sent Sennett to the South Side of Chicago to organize black workers. Here he found blacks exposed to the condescension and hostility of whites within the Communist Party; my uncle protested, and his local Party career suffered.[4] The American Communist Party dwelt upon the miseries of racism, particularly for black sharecropper-peasants in the American South; the Party saw these laborers as "natural" communists. With some honorable exceptions, the Party even so treated blacks as emblems of oppression rather than as actual human beings—a treatment dramatized in the later pages of Ralph Ellison's classic *Invisible Man*.

In the Spanish Civil War, Sennett was demoted as commissar of his army squadron by his own men, which he explains in his memoir as due to the fact that "I obviously had picked up the kind of bureaucratic approach that was a negative side of Communist leadership. I . . . conducted myself as a political leader in a very bureaucratic, dogmatic, and pompous fashion."[5]

Most markedly, he lacked a proper class consciousness. In the Blue Book, he recalls his view of the class struggle as a young Party organizer:

> I made a distinction between the working class and the bosses
> who were the wealthy, the upper classes, but I felt that the middle
> class, small business people, and professionals had more in com
> mon with working people than they did with the upper class.[6]

To make sense of this declaration, one has to recall that in the 1920s and 1930s the American Communist Party was the most ideologically rigid outside Russia. In large part the rigid outlook came from the Party's bourgeois members, who tended to loathe their own backgrounds; they were prone to idealize manual labor and the Heroic Worker. My uncle, who grew up in grinding poverty, had a more inclusive class consciousness— so inclusive, however, that it left almost no one out.

To understand my uncle's voice the reader must recall that McCarthyism in the 1950s had split the radical community apart like an ax. There were tormented souls like the journalist Whittaker Chambers who genuinely believed that the communist movement was a front for Russian spying and internal subversion. There was a large and diffuse group, spanning ex-communists to liberals like the historian Arthur Schlesinger, who were "anti-anticommunists," people who had renounced or rejected radical beliefs but attacked the puritanical purges led by Senator McCarthy on suspected radicals. And then there were people like my father—a dreamy, irresponsible man, his thoughts gravitating to the problems of translating modern Spanish poetry—accused of crimes they were incapable of committing.

In a memoir of his own youth, Schlesinger has declared that "only knaves or fools could defend Stalinism."[7] Certainly, the starring actor in my Family Romance was no paragon of political virtue; my uncle excused Stalin's pact with Hitler in 1939. But he was neither knave nor fool; his own life has a more sympathetic cast. He hadn't been seduced by his own riches; he practiced racial equality, harbored impulses of class inclusion and unbureaucratic behavior which damaged his communist career.

When I later came to know my uncle, he spoke critically of

the fancy titles I had chosen for my own books, pointing as a better model to a favored volume of his about the Jewish ghetto called *Life Is with People*. This could have served as the title of his own autobiography, except that the reader would never learn what it meant. He had a gut feeling for the "social" in the word "socialism." But it remained a gut feeling.

Though he does not use the phrase, I think my uncle struggled with the politics of respect. He believed from the outset of his career that capitalism emphasizing only the material status and prestige of individuals had little to offer across the divide of inequality. He discovered through bitter experience that the organized left of his time got in the way of mutual respect among comrades. It's this gut feeling that makes my uncle a kind of radical, humane Everyman.

Had I argued this sympathetic case to Brodsky he would, I'm sure, have had none of it. His life in Russia, like countless other lives, had been destroyed by people of whom the best that could be said was that they were misguided idealists.

The free pursuit of Brodsky's art led him to be treated with no respect by his tormentors; the way they expressed their contempt, however, was purely social. He had became the "misfit," *izgoy*. The totalitarian version of collective respect depended indeed, as Bourdieu observed among the Kabyle tribes, on an ideology in which the image of self is "indistinguishable . . . from that presented to other people."

Ex-communists like my uncle often assert that this repressive, conformist politics was a "historical error" resulting from the peculiarities of Russian society; others who turned against the entire body of Marxism have held their former ideals to account. The debate is clouded by intense personal feelings of betrayal and recrimination—but in one way it is a debate begun before the Soviet Union existed.

The bureaucratic pyramid, based on military procedures for the chain of command, appealed as much to some socialists at the end of the nineteenth century as it did to capitalists like John D. Rockefeller; from this form of bureaucracy Lenin would eventually derive the principles of a hierarchical vanguard Party with leaders in the vanguard functioning much like Rockefeller, quashing competition, imposing rigid discipline on those below. The socialist pyramid elicited a great debate at the end of the nineteenth century in Western Europe between Eduard Bernstein and Karl Kautsky. Bernstein rejected military organization as a model for unions, Kautsky thought nothing could be achieved without it; "democratic socialism," with its endless discussions and disputes, could be no recipe for effective revolution.[8]

Kautsky triumphed. In the international reach of Marxian socialism, the Party apparatus came to run as a military organization, top-down rather than bottom-up. It was this Western, militarized version of Party bureaucracy which was imported into Russia after the revolution, smothering other forms of indigenous radical practice. In the domestic sphere, the pyramid gave shape to Lenin's New Economic Policy of 1923–24. Stalin's social policy from the late 1920s onward consummated that passage; the dictator particularly admired the internal order which Henry Ford created in the company's massive motor works and conscientiously imitated it.

In one particular way Marxism could be held directly to

account for both my uncle's confusions and Brodsky's sufferings. This has to do with its framing of class consciousness. "In the West," the anthropologist Frank Henderson Stewart writes, "honor has usually been closely linked to the class system"; class makes the consciousness "vertical" rather than "horizontal," oriented to who stands above or below.[9] In the Marxian formula, awareness of those above or below comes before consciousness of those who are similar to oneself; inequality is prior to fraternity. The revolution's task is to make fraternity matter.

The assertion of class honor is a way for oppressed groups to do so, to take back control over their sense of collective self. For this reason, class consciousness has in Marxism an inherently military character: you cannot become truly aware of where you stand in the world without fighting the meanings others have imposed on your position. No class consciousness without class struggle: class enemies and friends will be revealed in their true colors during strikes or violent battles in the street; one's own real place in the world will be more clearly defined through combat. Ergo, Kautsky.

This taint is difficult even for democratic and humane modern Marxists such as Erik Olin Wright to remove. "If class as a concept is to explain anything, it must provide the basis for explaining class struggles, the formation of people into classes as organized forces," he asserts; "class [designates] the potential unity of such positions within the class struggle."[10]

The problem here is that any *positive* exchange with the enemy risks diminishing class solidarity. The adversarial model of class consciousness suffers the same problem faced by the Bororo, that of a paralyzing relationship between self and world. The surrender of tacit assumptions and behavior to a more exploratory relationship with others becomes difficult; it risks undoing of revolutionary will. Ambiguities of need, confusions of self, turning toward others unlike oneself—such traits of character have no place in this politics; they too would weaken the will to resist.

In the history of the communist movement, a kind of schizophrenia was therefore required, behavior which was aggressive and militaristic toward others, yet generous and mutually aware toward comrades—a magical passage which rarely occurred. In Spain, my uncle began to discover that political schizophrenia was not personally viable. His is one man's part of the larger story told in Orwell's *Homage to Catalonia*; "solidarity" had somehow to relate humanly to those, such as anarchists and uninvolved peasants, and even to priests and foot soldiers of the enemy, who differ.

By the time my uncle talked to the interviewers at the University of California, this was his dilemma: he hewed to the hatred of injustice and unequal power which had moved him as a young man, yet he wanted to break the bonds of orthodox class consciousness, to forge a more inclusive social bond.

The New Politics

Radicals in my own generation struggled as much as my uncle with problems of inclusion and mutual respect. They remained enemies of institutional capitalism but added to the enemies list institutional socialism. But making bureaucracy the enemy still did not reveal how to make friends with those who were not radicals.

The counterculture of the 1960s sometimes gave the impression of an endless party—nude swimming and LSD experiments punctuated by recreational protest. This cartoon masked a more serious conflict in my youth. Many of those who dropped out of established institutions fell into an aimless existence, moving from squat to squat, commune to commune. Many others, though, sought to remake the institutions they'd quit; they debated in a more engaged and serious way what was to be done. One of these engagements early on, in 1962, produced the Port Huron Statement, named after a small American town, the intimacy of the small town a hint of the contents of the manifesto. The Port Huron Statement was crafted by the young people who created Students for a Democratic Society, in search of a community more than an organization.[11]

Their manifesto has a moral fervor which perhaps marks its authors as American, and a sense of impending apocalypse which marks them as young. "We may be the last generation in the experiment with living," it declares, meaning that the New Left was struggling to free social life from capitalism's rigid embrace.[12] The young authors see themselves at the margins of a paralyzed society:

Feeling the press of complexity upon the emptiness of life, people are fearful . . . that at any moment things might be thrust out of control. . . . The dominant institutions are complex enough to blunt the minds of their potential critics. . . .[13]

Their overriding social fear is of the "loneliness, estrangement, isolation [which] describe the vast distance between man and man today."[14] These sentiments spoke for a young left not only in America but in Western Europe and Latin America. Nor would they have been foreign to my uncle's generation, particularly in their sense of estrangement from other people.

To be an American radical meant, however, inhabiting a marginal place in society. In the 1960s, as in the 1930s, when the left criticized the ills of society, it often touched a sympathetic chord among a large swath of the public; when it then proceeded to argue for fundamental change of the system, the public suddenly viewed it as an extremist sect.[15]

The New Left appealed to young people in other societies as well as America because it proposed a personalized version of community, anathema to the Old Left at home and abroad. The Port Huron Statement meant to the activist Richard Flacks "an exciting transformation of the meaning of socialism . . . it meant redefining the socialist tradition in terms of [its] democratic content," stressing direct, face-to-face participation.[16] Party discipline, bureaucratic control, had no place in these views. This institutional rejection reached beyond national borders. It marked many students on the streets of Paris in May 1968; among dissidents in Eastern Europe it played a powerful role in calls for "civil society," as in the writings and activism of the Hungarian George Konrad, who argued for an "antipolitics" of everyday social life.

The anti-institutional side of the New Left drove to distraction Old Leftists, for whom "cooperation" had long ceased to be an operative word; the little communes, the mutual heart-searching under the banner of "the personal is political," seemed to these hardened veterans just infantile self-indulgence. As soon as the Port Huron Statement was published in 1962 it generated a struggle between the League for Industrial Democracy—

anticommunist in ideology, rigid in temperament—and the looser young people in Students for a Democratic Society.

If one person embodied both sides of this debate it was the leader of SDS itself, Tom Hayden. Part of him was an institutional man, serving the antiwar cause as a canny bureaucratic operator; he forged a back-channel access to the American ambassador in Vietnam, Averell Harriman, at the same time he made open contacts with the North Vietnamese fighting the Americans, hoping, like all bureaucratic "players," to make himself indispensable to both. Part of Hayden was the appealing boy who dropped out of his own organization for months at a time, sleeping on the floors of filthy ghetto apartments, trying to release himself into the flux of everyday community life.

The passage of time validated in two ways the New Left's political critique of institutions. The first was our prediction of social atrophy of state socialism. When Timothy Garton Ash went to Budapest in 1990, interviewing people who had lived under a Marxist regime for forty years, he asked who Karl Marx was. People in Budapest's Marx Square told him the following:

> He was a Soviet Philosopher; Engels was his friend. Well, what else can I say? He died at an old age. (Another voice): Of course, a politician. And he was, you know, he was what's his name's—Lenin's, Lenin, Lenin's works—well he translated them into Hungarian.[17]

Disconnection and detachment marked the daily lives of ordinary citizens in the Soviet empire, especially in its outposts; spectatorship became a way of survival. In politics, Leszek Kolakowski notes:

The great majority voted in the sham elections to avoid unpleasant consequences, though not very serious ones; they took part in the obligatory marches. . . . The police informers were easily recruited, won over by miserable privileges.[18]

Decay and apathy marked the system; at the heart of the empire, Gorbachev attacked the era of *zastoy*, "stagnation." The New Left was a prescient and trenchant critic of just this illness.

The historical irony of my generation, secondly, was that capitalism made New Left desires come half true. The attack on the bureaucratic pyramid in favor of disk organization often succeeded in destroying the institutional rigidities of the old order, in public institutions as well as private ones. The shift from bureaucratic to flexible capitalism reinforced the emphasis on voluntary social action and on face-to-face relations in civil society. The ideology of flexibility emphasized risk-taking and spontaneity, the life narrative set free from a determinate course.

The fact that capitalism has done the work the New Left wanted does not invalidate the New Left's radical impulse. It would have been hard forty years ago, in the Age of the Organization Man, to see the social consequences of disorganization. We hoped the dismantling of fixed bureaucracy would promote stronger social connections between people. Our faith lay in improvisation, in social relations which more resembled jazz than classical music. As it turns out, social jazz did not bring more sociability.

In our own time we had an inkling of this. The struggle to break apart institutions failed to bring the New Left closer to people unlike ourselves. The New Left had a hostile relationship to what by 1970 in America was called the "silent majority," the white working-class or lower-middle-class ordinary people. The silent majority was more outraged than silent, as I learned in Boston, in the same years when New York construction workers attacked peace demonstrators as liberal elitists.

The workers were partly right: an often unthinking snobbism pervaded the ranks of privileged radicals. Yet the proletariat remained an object of radical desire. Old Marxist songs of explaining to the proletariat its true class position continued to be sung. And just because the basic critical impulses of the New Left addressed real social evils, decent young people caught in this bind felt they couldn't make themselves understood. The Port Huron Statement could speak about institutions being out of touch with ordinary people, but so were we.

My generation wound up facing the same dilemma of older people in social relations: goodwill combined with improvisation—social jazz—does not bind.

Conclusion

This essay has shifted, I know, between the extremes of concrete experience and social theory, leaving in the gap policies and plans. In part the account I've given is a caution against filling that gap. Treating people with respect cannot occur simply by commanding it should happen. Mutual recognition has to be negotiated; this negotiation engages the complexities of personal character as much as social structure.

Social solutions seem more apparent in considering the inequalities which tarnish the three modern codes of respect: make something of yourself, take care of yourself, help others.

The tarnish could be removed, somewhat, by honoring differing practical achievements rather than privileging potential talent; by admitting the just claims of adult dependency; by permitting people to participate more actively in the conditions of their own care.

As I have tried to show, each of these principles has a concrete application in the welfare system; all three would increase rather than make more scarce mutual respect between doctors and patients, the managers and residents of public housing, and social workers and their clients.

What practical policy cannot do is remove the fundamental discomfort which inequality arouses in modern society. The British sociologist T. H. Marshall drew the ire of doctrinaire Marxists for plain speaking on this score. He was politically correct in proclaiming that the British welfare state constructed after the Second World War aimed to replace the "differential status, associated with class, function and family, . . . by the single uniform status of citizenship." But Marshall completed his thought by asserting that these social rights "provided the foundation of equality on which the structure of inequality could be built."[19] There are, he believed, unavoidable inequalities.

This was the view even of R. H. Tawney, who was never the simple egalitarian he is sometimes made out to be. In *Equality,* Tawney forthrightly declared that

> to criticize inequality and to desire equality is not, as is sometimes suggested, to cherish the romantic illusion that men are equal in character and intelligence. It is to hold that, while their natural endowments differ profoundly, it is the mark of a civilized society to aim at eliminating such inequalities as

have their source, not in individual differences but in [social] organization. . . .[20]

In no conceivable way could Tawney or Marshall be read as apologists for inequality. Their aim is to test its necessity— when and where it can be avoided, when and where it must be accepted.

These tests may yield unwanted results. My family made an experiment in searching for greater social respect; my own life has been in part an exploration of the foundations of self-respect. Inequality, experienced as the divide between the strong and the weak, played a disturbing role in both.

The kind of equality I have affirmed in this book is founded on the psychology of autonomy. Rather than an equality of understanding, autonomy means accepting in others what one does not understand about them. In so doing, the fact of their autonomy is treated as equal to your own. The grant of autonomy dignifies the weak or the outsider; to make this grant to others in turn strengthens one's own character.

I suppose this is as much of a moral as I can find in refelcting on the experience of my family and my peers. Probably their confusions signified more. Distressed by unjust inequalities, determined to treat others well, neither generation of radicals found a remedy; neither sheer goodwill nor institutional leveling would provide an answer to treating others with respect. My own experiences led by a different route to the same difficulty. I was less politically engaged than my uncle or my peers, and the inequalities in my life took form in relation to Cabrini, the circumstances of my life departing unimaginably from those who remained.

They and I have unfinished business, though this business can only be conducted in memory: I departed, but have tried to return, in this book.

If there is any conclusion I can draw from my own experience, it is that self-respect founded on craft cannot alone generate mutual respect. In society, attacking the evils of inequality cannot alone generate mutual respect. In society, and particularly in the welfare state, the nub of the problem we face is how the strong can practice respect toward those destined to remain weak. Performing arts like music reveal the collaboative elements in the expressive practice of mutual respect; the stubborn facts of division remain society's problem.

Notes

Chapter 1: Memories of Cabrini

1. Alex Kotlowitz, *There Are No Children Here* (New York: Anchor, 1991), p. 24.
2. Gloria Hayes Morgan, "Another Time, Another Place," *Chicago Tribune Magazine,* December 13, 1992, p. 14.
3. David Whitaker, *Cabrini Green in Words and Pictures* (Chicago: W3 Publishers in affiliation with LPC Group, 2000), p. 5.
4. Dorothy Sennett, "The Project" (unpublished, 1959), p. 3. A good comprehensive look at the community is Larry Bennett, "Communitarian Thinking and the Redevelopment of Chicago's Cabrini-Green Public Housing Complex," *Journal of Urban Affairs* 20 (2): 99–116.
5. Cf. A. Donajgrodzki, ed., *Social Control in 19th Century Britain* (Totowa, N.J.: Rowman & Littlefield, 1977), pp. 9ff.
6. Sennett, "The Project," p. 1.
7. Ibid., p. 2.
8. Ibid., p. 1.
9. The contrast between the two parts of Chicago, before Cabrini was built, was explored in Harvey Zorbaugh, *The Gold Coast and the Slum,* originally published in 1929, reprinted in 1983 (Chicago: University of Chicago Press, 1983).
10. Morgan, p. 15.
11. Whitaker, p. 13.

12. Sennett, "The Project," pp. 3–4.
13. Dalton Conley, *Honky* (Berkeley: University of California Press, 2000), p. 37.
14. Dorothy Sennett, "A Perpetual Holiday" (unpublished, 1959), p. 2.
15. Ibid.
16. Marshall Berman, *All That Is Solid Melts into Air* (New York: Penguin USA, 1988), p. 121.
17. James Miller, *Democracy Is in the Streets: From Port Huron to the Siege of Chicago* (Cambridge, Mass.: Harvard University Press, 1994), p. 147.
18. The book is Richard Sennett, *Families Against the City: Middle-Class Homes of Industrial Chicago* (Cambridge, Mass.: Harvard University Press, 1970).
19. The major mentoring organizations were Project Education Plus, known as PREP; Cabrini Connections, which used adults; and CYCLE, a tutoring and mentoring program using Wheaton College students.
20. An abbreviated account of this meeting appeared in the *New York Times*, during the confirmation hearings of Clarence Thomas for the U.S. Supreme Court; Judge Thomas was held up by his supporters as a role model for the poor. See my op-ed in the *New York Times*, August 12, 1991, p. A15.
21. The best general description of this dilemma I know is William Julius Wilson, *When Work Disappears: The World of the New Urban Poor* (New York: Vintage, 1997).
22. I have changed his profession in the interest of privacy.
23. See Philip Augar, *The Death of Gentlemanly Capitalism* (London: Penguin, 2000).
24. Richard Sennett and Jonathan Cobb, *The Hidden Injuries of Class* (New York: Knopf, 1972).

Chapter 2: What Respect Means

1. Currently available on disk on Polygram #445188, titled *Erlkönig: The Art of the Lied*.
2. Dietrich Fischer-Dieskau, *The Fischer-Dieskau Song-book* (London: Faber & Faber, 1993).
3. Michael Ignatieff, *The Needs of Strangers* (New York: Viking, 1985).
4. Hans Gerth and C. Wright Mills, *Character and Social Structure: The Psychology of Institutions* (New York: Harcourt Brace, 1953).
5. Pierre Bourdieu, "The Sentiment of Honour in Kabyle Society," trans. Philip Sherrard, in J. G. Péristiany, ed., *Honour and Shame: The Values*

of Mediterranean Society (Chicago: University of Chicago Press, 1966), p. 211.

6. Ibid.; the phrase is *Argaz sirgazen; Rabbi imanis.*

7. Judith Shklar, *American Citizenship: The Quest for Inclusion* (Cambridge, Mass.: Harvard University Press, 1995). See particularly Pt. 1.

8. Nancy Fraser and Linda Gordon, "A Genealogy of Dependency," *Signs,* Winter 1994, p. 324.

Chapter 3: Unequal Talent

1. Emmanuel Le Roy Ladurie, *St.-Simon and the Court of Louis XIV,* trans. Arthur Goldhammer (Chicago: University of Chicago Press, 2001), p. 46.

2. Samuel Pepys, *Diaries,* ed. Robert Latham (London: Penguin, 1993), p. 375.

3. Sir John Fortesque, *De Laudibus Legem Angliae,* ed. S. B. Chrimes (Cambridge, U.K.: Cambridge University Press, 1942), pp. 31–32.

4. Le Roy Ladurie, pp. 59–60.

5. Cited in Nicholas Lemann, *The Big Test: The Secret History of American Meritocracy* (New York: Farrar, Straus & Giroux, 1999), p. 43.

6. Mary Poovey, *A History of the Modern Fact* (Chicago: University of Chicago Press, 1998).

7. A vivid account of these trials appears in Fintan O'Toole, *A Traitor's Kiss* (London: Granta, 1998), pp. 172–75.

8. See William G. Bowen and Derek Bok, *The Shape of the River: Long-Term Consequences of Considering Race in College and University Admissions* (Princeton, N.J.: Princeton University Press, 1998).

9. David McClelland, *The Achieving Society* (Princeton, N.J.: Van Nostrand, 1961), pp. 205–58.

10. Philip Brown and Hugh Lauder, *Capitalism and Social Progress* (Basingstoke: Palgrave, 2001), p. 215.

11. Robert Reich, *The Work of Nations: Preparing Ourselves for 21st Century Capitalism* (New York: Knopf, 1991).

12. See Saskia Sassen, *Globalization and Its Discontents* (New York: The New Press, 1998), Chapter 1.

13. See Christopher Jencks, *Who Gets Ahead* (New York: Basic Books, 1979), Chapters 4 and 5.

14. W. H. Auden, *Collected Poems,* ed. Edward Mendelson (New York: Random House, 1976), pp. 629–33.

15. See Thorstein Veblen, *The Theory of the Leisure Class* (New Brunswick, N.J.: Transaction, 1992).

16. Jean-Jacques Rousseau, *Discourse on the Origin of Inequality,* in *The*

Collected Writings of Rousseau, ed. Roger D. Masters and Christopher Kelly (Hanover, N.H.: University Press of New England, 1991), 3:91, note 12.

17. Maurice Cranston, *The Noble Savage,* vol.2 of *The Life of Jean-Jacques Rousseau* (Chicago: University of Chicago Press, 1991), p. 304.

18. Jean-Jacques Rousseau, *Discourse on the Origin of Inequality,* ed. Maurice Cranston (New York: Penguin Books, 1984), p. 114.

19. Friedrich Nietzsche, *Beyond Good and Evil,* trans. Walter Kaufmann (New York: Vintage, 1966), #221.

20. Adam Smith, *The Wealth of Nations,* (1776; London: Methuen, 1961), pp. 107, 109.

21. Adam Ferguson, *An Essay on the History of Civil Society* (New York: Cambridge University Press, 1996), p. 364.

22. I am particularly indebted in this reading of Rousseau to Marshall Berman, *The Politics of Authenticity* (New York: Atheneum, 1970).

23. Ronald Dworkin, *Sovereign Virtue: The Theory and Practice of Equality* (Cambridge, Mass.: Harvard University Press, 2000), pp. 326–27.

24. Howard Gardner, *Frame of Mind: The Theory of Multiple Intelligences* (New York: Basic Books, 1983).

25. Amartya Sen, "Economic Development and Social Change: India and China in Comparative Perspectives," London School of Economics STICERD Discussion Paper Series, December 1995.

26. Lemann, p. 347.

27. Michael Young, *The Rise of the Meritocracy, 1870–2033* (Piscataway, N.J.: Transaction, 1999), p. 179.

28. See Paul Willis, *Learning to Labor: How Working Class Kids Get Working Class Jobs* (New York: Columbia University Press, 1981).

Chapter 4: The Shame of Dependence

1. Tony Blair, "Address to the Labour Party Annual Conference, 1997," text courtesy Prime Minister's Press Office, p. 12.

2. Daniel Patrick Moynihan, *The Politics of a Guaranteed Income* (New York: Random House, 1973), p. 17.

3. Immanuel Kant, "An Answer to the Question: 'What Is Enlightenment,' " in *Kant's Political Writings,* trans. H. B. Nisbet (Cambridge, U.K.: Cambridge University Press, 1970), p. 54.

4. For a useful commentary on Locke's opponents, see Gordon Schochet, *Patriarchalism in Political Thought* (New York: Basic Books, 1975).

5. John Locke, *The Second Treatise of Government,* ed. Thomas Peardon (New York: Macmillan, 1986), p. 37.

6. "Individualism" appears in the second volume of Alexis de Tocqueville,

Democracy in America, ed. J. P. Mayer, trans. George Lawrence (New York: Harper & Row, 1988). Margaret Thatcher, interview with Douglas Keay, *Women's Own* magazine, October 31, 1987, p. 8.

7. Locke, pp. 41ff.

8. Etienne de La Boétie, "On Voluntary Servitude," trans. David Lewis Schaefer, in *Freedom over Servitude: Montaigne, La Boétie, and "On Voluntary Servitude,"* ed. David Lewis Schaefer (Westport, Conn.: Greenwood Press, 1998), pp. 191–94.

9. Dostoevsky, *The Brothers Karamazov,* "The Grand Inquisitor," no. 11, pp. 288ff. (London: Penquin, 1958).

10. See Judith N. Shklar, *American Citizenship* (Cambridge, Mass.: Harvard University Press, 1991).

11. See Johann Huizinga, *Homo Ludens* (Boston: Beacon Press, 1955), conclusion.

12. Nancy Fraser and Linda Gordon, "A Genealogy of Dependency," *Signs,* Winter 1994, p. 317.

13. Philippe Ariès, *Centuries of Childhood* (New York: Vintage, 1964).

14. David Whitaker, *Cabrini Green in Words and Pictures* (Chicago: W3 Publishers in affiliation with LPC Group, 2000), p. 210.

15. See Sigmund Freud, "Fragment of an Analysis of Hysteria," *Case Histories,* vol. I (Harmondsworth: Penquin, 1977).

16. See Ronald Dore, *City Life in Japan* (London: Routledge & Kegan Paul, 1958).

17. Takeo Doi, *The Anatomy of Dependence,* trans. John Bester (New York: Kodansha Publishers, 1977), p. 20.

18. The passage, which I believe comes originally from G. F. Hegel's *Theologische Jugendschriften,* is quoted in Ludwig Bingswanger, *und Erkenntnis menschlichen Daseins* (Zurich: Max Niehaus, 1942), p. 508. My translation.

19. See Gerhart Piers and Milton Singer, *Shame and Guilt* (New York: W. W. Norton, 1971), pp. 48–52.

20. See Richard Sennett, *Authority* (New York: Knopf, 1980), Chapters 1 and 3.

21. As in so many things, I am indebted to Gerhart Piers for this reference. See Piers and Singer, p. 18, for a fuller etymology of the word.

22. Erik Erikson, *Identity and the Life Cycle* (New York: W. W. Norton, 1980), p. 71.

23. Sylvan Tomkins, *Shame and Its Sisters* (Durham, N.C.: Duke University Press, 1995), p. 137.

24. Niklas Luhmann, "Familiarity, Confidence, Trust" in Diego Gambetta, ed., *Trust* (Oxford: Blackwell, 1988), p. 102.

25. Personal communication. Dumont's work on India is best represented in Louis Dumont, *Homo Hierarchicus* (Chicago: University of Chicago, 1966).
26. Erikson, p. 70.
27. Ibid.
28. See D. W. Winnicott, *Collected Papers,* vol. 1; "Transitional Objects," pp. 229–42 (London: Tavistock, 1958). John Bowlby, *Separation* (London: Hogarth Press, 1973).
29. Adam Smith, *The Theory of Moral Sentiments* (Indianapolis: Liberty Fund Press, 1982), p. 21.
30. Locke, p. 95.
31. Annette Weiner, *Inalienable Possessions: The Paradox of Keeping-While-Giving* (Berkeley: University of California Press, 1992), p. 31. See Durkheim directly in Emile Durkheim, *The Division of Labor in Society,* trans. W. D. Halls (New York: Free Press, 1984), pp. 21–22.

Chapter 5: **Compassion Which Wounds**

1. See Gertrude Himmelfarb, *Poverty and Compassion: The Moral Imagination of the Late Victorians* (New York: Knopf, 1991).
2. Quoted in Mary Louis Sullivan, *Mother Cabrini* (New York: Center for Migration Studies, 1992), p. 49.
3. Quoted by Jane Addams in "A Modern Lear," *Survey Magazine,* Nov. 2, 1912. I am unable to trace the source further, but use it, as will appear, as part of Addams's own views.
4. Quoted in Michael Katz, *In the Shadow of the Poorhouse* (New York: Basic Books, 1986), p. 76.
5. The best description of Addams's work is to be found in Allen Davis, *American Heroine: The Life and Legend of Jane Addams* (New York: Oxford University Press, 1975).
6. Addams, "A Modern Lear."
7. Daniel Rodgers, *Atlantic Crossings: Social Politics in a Progressive Age* (Cambridge, Mass.: Belknap Press, 1998), p. 11.
8. Sullivan, p. 143.
9. Sullivan, p. 45.
10. Sullivan, Appendix C, p. 261.
11. Natan Sznaider, *The Compassionate Temperament* (Oxford: Rowman & Littlefield, 2001), p. 96.
12. Jean Starobinski, *Largesse,* trans. Jane Marie Todd (Chicago: University of Chicago Press, 1997), p. 15.
13. Georges Bataille, *La part maudite: précédé de la notion de dépense* (Paris: Editions de Minuit, 1967), pp. 27–28.

14. William Wordsworth, "The Old Cumberland Beggar," in *Poems*, ed. John Hayden (London: Penguin, 1977), stanza 6.
15. Suetonius, "Nero," in *The Twelve Caesars* (London: Penguin, 1991), p. 247. I owe to Jean Starobinski this and the following reference.
16. Antonin Artaud, "Heliogabale ou l'anarchiste couronneé," in *Oeuvres complètes* (Paris: Gallimard, 1970), 7:102–3.
17. Etienne de La Boétie, *The Politics of Obedience: The Discourse of Voluntary Servitude*, trans. Harry Kurz (Montreal: Black Rose, 1975), p. 70.
18. Hannah Arendt, *Love and Saint Augustine*, ed. and trans. Joanna Vecchiarelli Scott and Judith Chelius Stark (Chicago: University of Chicago Press, 1996), p. 95.
19. Ibid., p. 97.
20. The Gospel According to St. Matthew 6:1,3–4 (King James version).
21. St. Augustine, *The Confessions*, trans. Henry Chadwick (New York: Oxford University Press, 1998), X, 33, 50.
22. See Philippe Van Parijs, *Real Freedom for All* (Oxford: Oxford University Press, 1998).
23. Quoted in Richard Sennett, *Flesh and Stone* (New York: W. W. Norton, 1994), p. 158.
24. Nancy Chodorow, *The Reproduction of Mothering* (Berkeley: University of California Press, 1978), p. 167.
25. Carol Gilligan, *In a Different Voice* (Cambridge, Mass: Harvard University Press, 1993), p. 17.
26. Scott and Stark, "Rediscovering Hannah Arendt," in Arendt, *Love and Saint Augustine*, p. 137.
27. Quoted in Elizabeth Young-Bruehl, *Hannah Arendt: For Love of the World* (New Haven, Conn.: Yale University Press, 1982), p. 455.
28. See Stanley Cohen, *States of Denial* (Cambridge, U.K.: Polity, 2001). The defense mechanism is traced on pp. 52–58.
29. W. H. Auden, "Musée des Beaux Arts," in *Collected Poems*, ed. Edward Mendelson (New York: Random House, 1976), pp. 146–47.
30. Quoted in Wolfgang Stechow, *Brueghel* (New York: Abrams, 1990), p. 51.
31. Hannah Arendt, *On Revolution* (New York: Viking, 1963), pp. 74–75.

Chapter 6: Bureaucratic Respect

1. A useful summary of these statistics appears in Jan van der Ploeg and Evert Scholte, *Homeless Youth* (London: Sage, 1997), pp. 16–18.
2. Erving Goffman, *Asylums* (New York: Anchor, 1961); Peter Townsend, *The Last Refuge* (London: Routledge & Kegan Paul, 1962).

3. Michel Foucault, *Discipline and Punish*, trans. Alan Sheridan (New York: Vintage, 1995).

4. R. A. Parker, "Residential Care for Children," in Ian Sinclair, ed., *Residential Care* (London: HMSO, 1988), pp. 70–71.

5. Katherine Jones, *Asylums and After* (London: Athlone, 1993), pp. 220–22.

6. See J. L. Powers et al., "Maltreatment Among Runaway and Homeless Youth," *Child Abuse and Neglect* 14 (1990): 87–98.

7. John Pitts, *Working with Young Offenders,* 2nd ed. (London: Macmillan, 1999), p. 12.

8. Cf. Peter Mandelson and Roger Liddle, *The Blair Revolution* (London: Faber, 1996).

9. Henry James, *The American Scene,* in *Writing New York,* ed. Philip Lopate (New York: Library of America, 1998), p. 372.

10. Harold Macmillan, *The Middle Way* (1938; reprinted London: Macmillan, 1966), p. 108.

11. See Robert Wiebe, *The Search for Order: 1877–1920* (New York: Hill & Wang, 1967); also Olivier Zunz, *Making America Corporate: 1870–1920* (Chicago: University of Chicago Press, 1990).

12. In these numbers, I have excluded agricultural activity, which shows the same trend but in another way. *Historical Statistics of the U.S. from Colonial Times to 1970* (U.S. Bureau of the Census, 1975).

13. Max Weber, "Parliament and Government in Germany Under a New Political Order" (1918), trans. and ed. P. Lassman and R. Speirs, in Weber, *Political Writings* (Cambridge, U.K.: Cambridge University Press, 1994), p. 145.

14. See Olivier Zunz, particularly Zunz's comparative analysis of the creation of the Du Pont and Ford corporations, pp. 68ff.

15. Max Weber, *The Protestant Ethic and the Spirit of Capitalism,* trans. Talcott Parsons (New York: HarperCollins Academic, 1991), p. 181.

16. See Irving Bernstein, *The Lean Years* (New York: Penguin, 1966), pp. 23ff.

17. Theda Skocpol, *Protecting Soldiers and Mothers: The Political Origins of Social Policy in the U.S.* (Cambridge, Mass.: Belknap Press, 1992).

18. Gösta Esping-Anderson, *The Three Worlds of Welfare Capitalism* (Princeton, N.J.: Princeton University Press, 1990).

19. See Emma Rothschild, "Who's Going to Pay for All This?" (review of Nancy Folbre, *The Invisible Heart*), *New York Times Book Review,* July 1, 2001.

20. See Nick Clegg, report on OECD social services spending summarized in "Lessons from Europe," *Guardian,* July 23, 2001, p. 18

21. Gloria Hayes Morgan, "Another Time, Another Place," *Chicago Tribune Magazine,* December 13, 1992, p. 14.
22. See Albert Hirschmann, *Exit, Voice and Loyalty: Responses to Declines in Firms, Organizations, and States* (Cambridge, Mass.: Harvard University Press, 1970).
23. David Whitaker, *Cabrini Green in Words and Pictures* (Chicago: W3 Publishers in affiliation with LPC Group, 2000), p. 99.
24. Gordon Burke, *Housing and Social Justice* (New York: Longman, 1981) p. 4.
25. Quoted in I. Shaw, S. Lambert, and D. Clapham, *Social Care and Housing* (London: Kingsley, 1998), p. 91.
26. See Richard Cloward and Frances Fox Piven, *Regulating the Poor: Functions of Public Welfare* (New York: Pantheon, 1971), especially pp. 248–84.
27. John Maynard Keynes, quoted in D. E. Moggridge, *Keynes* (London: Macmillan, 1980), p. 80.
28. An excellent discussion of "the middle way" is to be found in Vic George and Paul Wilding, *Welfare and Ideology* (New York: Harvester, 1994), pp. 46–73.
29. Burke, p. 6.

Chapter 7: Liberated Welfare

1. Robert Skidelsky, *John Maynard Keynes,* vol. 1 (London: Macmillan, 1983; "Papermac" reprint, 1992), pp. 185–86.
2. Amit Chaudhuri, "Freedom Song," in Chaudhuri, *Three Novels* (London: Picador, 2001), p. 296.
3. See Saskia Sassen, *The Global City* (Princeton, N.J.: Princeton University Press, 1991).
4. Laurie Graham, *On the Line at Subaru-Isuzu: The Japanese Model and the American Worker* (Ithaca, N.Y.: ILR Press, 1995).
5. John Kotter, *The New Rules: How To Succeed in Today's Post-Corporate World* (New York: Free Press, 1995), p. 159.
6. See Robert Frank, *The Winner-Take-All Society* (New York: Free Press, 1995).
7. Patrick Dunleavy, "The Political Implications of Sectoral Cleavages and the Growth of State Employment," *Political Studies* 28 (1980): 364–84, 527–49.
8. Bob Jessop, *Conservative Regimes and the Transition to Post-Fordism* (Colchester, U.K.: University of Essex Papers, 1988), p. 29. See also Christopher Pierson, *Beyond the Welfare State?,* 2nd ed. (London: Polity Press, 1999), pp. 61–62.

9. Andrew Grove, *Only the Paranoid Survive* (New York: Doubleday, 1996), p. 6.

10. Richard Sennett, *The Corrosion of Character* (New York: W. W. Norton, 1998), p. 25.

11. Robert Putnam, *Bowling Alone* (New York: Simon & Schuster, 2000), pp. 87, 91.

12. See Charles Hecksher, *White-Collar Blues: Management Loyalties in an Age of Corporate Restructuring* (New York: Basic Books, 1995).

13. Fraser and Gordon, ibid.

14. Jeremy Rifkin, *The End of Work* (New York: Putnam, 1995); Robert Howard, *Brave New Workplace* (New York: Viking Penquin, 1985).

15. For an excellent discussion of such programs, see John Pitts, *Working with Young Offenders*, 2nd ed. (London: Macmillan, 1999), pp. 110–13.

16. John Calvin, *Institutes of the Christian Religion*, ed. John T. McNeill, trans. Ford Lewis Battles (Philadelphia: Westminster Press, 1960).

17. William Wordsworth, "The Old Cumberland Beggar," in *Poems,* ed. John Hayden (London: Penguin, 1977), 1:262–68.

18. Patrick Collinson, "Holy-Rowly-Powliness," *London Review of Books,* Jan. 4, 2001, p. 33. See also Adam Fox, *Oral and Literate Culture in England, 1500–1700* (Oxford: Oxford University Press, 2000).

19. See Putnam, pp. 130–31. Putnam's conclusion: "Volunteering that can be done by senior citizens, such as youth mentoring, is up. Volunteering that requires a younger constitution, such as . . . giving blood, is down."

20. See Putnam, op. cit., pp 50–58.

21. See Robert Wuthnow, *Acts of Compassion* (Princeton, N.J.: Princeton University Press, 1991).

22. Sherryl Kleinman and Gary Alan Fine, "Rhetorics and Action in Moral Organization" *Urban Life* 8 (3) (1979): 279–94.

23. Putnam, p. 22.

24. See Vanessa Martlew, "Transfusion Medicine," in Richard Titmuss, *The Gift Relationship: From Human Blood to Social Policy,* expanded and updated version with new chapters by others (New York: Free Press, 1997), p. 50.

25. See *Comprehensive Report on Blood Collection and Transfusion in the United States* (Bethesda, Md.: National Blood Data Resource Center, 1999), pp. 29ff.

26. Richard Titmuss, *The Gift Relationship* (New York: Vintage, 1972), pp. 129, 141.

27. See also Michael Ignatieff, *The Needs of Strangers* (New York: Viking, 1985).

28. Gillian Weaver and A. Susan Williams, "A Mother's Gift," a paper reproduced in the expanded version of Titmuss, p. 13.
29. Abram de Swann, *In Care of the State* (New York: Oxford, 1988), pp. 253–55. See also Theda Skocpol and Morris Fiorina, "Making Sense of the Civic Engagement Debate," in Skocpol and Fiorina, *Civic Engagement in American Society* (New York: Russell Sage Foundation, 1999), pp. 1–23.
30. Quoted in Iain Boyd White, "Design and Class," *Harvard Design Magazine* 11 (Summer 2000): 22.

Chapter 8: The Mutual in Mutual Respect

1. Quoted in Natalie Davis, *The Gift in Sixteenth-Century France* (Oxford: Oxford University Press, 2000), p. 20.
2. My source for this is frustrating; the scene described here was recounted to me by the late biographer of Voltaire Theodore Besterman, but I can find no written report of it, and so report it only as hearsay.
3. See Joan Chissell, "Introduction" to Johannes Brahms, Quintet for Clarinet and Strings in B Minor, Op. 115 (London: Eulenburg, 1982), n.p. All references to the score use the Eulenburg edition, which is an urtext printing.
4. Richard Sennett, *Flesh and Stone* (New York: W. W. Norton, 1994), p. 310.
5. Peter Berger, "On the Obsolescence of the Concept of Honor," in *Revision: Changing Perspectives in Moral Philosophy,* eds. Stanley Hauerwas and Alasdair MacIntyre (Notre Dame: University of Notre Dame Press, 1983), p. 177.
6. Bronislaw Malinowski, *Argonauts of the Western Pacific* (London: Routledge & Kegan Paul, 1922).
7. Ibid., pp. 473ff.
8. Annette Weiner, *Inalienable Possessions* (Berkeley: University of California Press, 1992), p. 43.
9. I am indebted to Natalie Zemon Davis for all these references; see Davis, *The Gift in Sixteenth Century France* (Oxford: Oxford University Press, 2000), pp. 10–11.
10. Marcel Mauss, *The Gift,* trans. W. D. Halls (London: Routledge, 1990), p. 67.
11. Mary Douglas, "No Free Gifts," foreword to Mauss, p. vii.
12. Ibid., p. xvi.
13. Alain Caillé, *Anthropologie du Don* (Paris: Desclée de Brouwer, 2000), pp. 205–10.

14. See Pierre Bourdieu, "The Sentiment of Honour in Kabyle Society," trans. Philip Sherrard, in J. G. Péristiany, ed., *Honour and Shame: The Values of Mediterranean Society* (Chicago: University of Chicago Press, 1966), pp. 193–94.

15. Elijah Anderson, *Code of the Street* (New York: W. W. Norton, 1999), pp. 290–325.

16. Adam Seligman, *The Problem of Trust* (Princeton, N.J.: Princeton University Press, 1997), p. 54.

17. Frank Henderson Stewart, *Honor* (Chicago: University of Chicago Press, 1994), p. 51.

Chapter 9: A Character Turned Outward

1. Claude Levi-Strauss, *Tristes Tropiques,* trans. John and Doreen Weightman (New York: Modern Library, 1997), p. 249.

2. Ibid.

3. I owe this example to the pianist Alfred Brendel, who presented it in a remarkable series of lectures he gave in New York's Carnegie Hall in 1997.

4. See Beethoven, *32 Piano Sonatas,* ed. Artur Schnabel (New York: Simon & Schuster, 1935), vol. 2. The passages cited are the first eight bars of variation two (p. 780) versus the first two bars of variation six (p. 789).

5. John Seely Brown and Paul Duguid, *The Social Life of Information* (Cambridge, Mass.: Harvard Business School Press, 2000), p. 203.

6. Ibid., p. 205.

7. Michael Polanyi, *Knowing and Being* (London: Routledge & Kegan Paul, 1969), p. 5.

8. M. M. Bakhtin, *The Dialogic Imagination: Four Essays,* ed. Michael Holquist, trans. Caryl Emerson and Michael Holquist (Austin: University of Texas Press, 1981), p. 428.

9. Maurice Merleau-Ponty, in Maurice A. Natanson, ed., *Phenomenology and The Social Sciences* (Evanston, Ill.: Northwestern University Press, 1973).

10. The problem of projection is well described in Joseph Rykwert, *The Idea of a Town* (Cambridge, Mass.: MIT Press, 1980).

11. Sigmund Freud, *Civilization and Its Discontents,* trans. James Strachey (New York: W. W. Norton, 1961), p. 18.

12. John Dewey, *Art as Experience* (1934; New York: Capricorn, 1959), p. 15.

13. John Locke, *Essay Concerning Human Understanding*, ed. A. C. Fraser (New York: Dover, 1959) vol. 1, pp. 458–59.

14. David Hume, "The Treatise of Human Nature," in *The Philosophy of David Hume*, ed. V. C. Chappell (New York: Modern Library, 1963), p. 176.

15. See Anna Freud, *The Ego and the Mechanisms of Defense* (New York: International Publishers, 1967).

16. Henry Petroski, *The Evolution of Useful Things* (New York: Knopf, 1992), pp. 22–33.

17. See Richard Sennett, *Flesh and Stone* (New York: W. W. Norton, 1994), pp. 212–51.

18. Daniel Kahneman and Amos Tversky, "Prospect Theory: An Analysis of Decision Under Risk," *Econometrica* 47 (2) (1979): 263–91.

19. William Hazlitt, *Essay on the Principles of Human Action*, quoted in A. C. Grayling, *The Quarrel of the Age* (London: Weidenfeld & Nicolson, 2000).

20. Erich Auerbach, *Mimesis* (Princeton, N.J.: Princeton University Press, 1953), p. 459.

21. Ibid.

Chapter 10: The Politics of Respect

1. William Sennett, *Communist Functionary and Corporate Executive*, an oral history conducted 1981 and 1982 by Marshall Windmiller (Berkeley: Regional Oral History Office, Bancroft Library, University of California, 1984).

2. Ibid., p. 372.

3. See David Bethea, *Joseph Brodsky and the Creation of Exile* (Princeton, N.J.: Princeton University Press, 1994), pp. 37, 87.

4. See William Sennett, pp. 37–42.

5. Ibid., p. 95.

6. Ibid., p. 27.

7. Arthur Schlesinger, Jr., *A Life in the 20th Century* (Boston: Houghton Mifflin, 2000), p. 401.

8. See Norman Birnbaum, *After Progress* (New York: Oxford University Press, 2001), pp. 30–32. This is a superb book, more largely, on the politics of modern socialism.

9. Frank Henderson Stewart, *Honor* (Chicago: University of Chicago Press, 1994), p. 130.

10. Erik Olin Wright, "Varieties of Marxist Conceptions of Class Structure," *Politics and Society* 9 (1980): 339.

11. In the passages quoted below, the text used is "The Port Huron Statement" as reprinted as the appendix to James Miller, *Democracy Is in the Streets*, rev. ed. (Cambridge, Mass.: Harvard University Press, 1994).

The statement was drafted in Port Huron, Michigan, June 11–15, 1962.

12. Ibid., p. 330.

13. Ibid.

14. Ibid., p. 332.

15. See Seymour Martin Lipset and Gary Marks, *It Didn't Happen Here* (New York: W. W. Norton, 2000). The authors emphasize, it should be said, political factors more than societal aspirations.

16. Quoted in Miller, p. 145.

17. Timothy Garton Ash, *The Uses of Adversity* (New York: Vintage, 1990), p. 261.

18. Leszek Kolakowsi, "Amidst Moving Ruins," *Daedalus* 121 (2) (1992): 55–56.

19. T. H. Marshall and Thomas Bottomore, *Citizenship and Social Class* (London: Pluto, 1992), p. 21. The book elaborates Marshall's basic text, *Citizenship and Social Class* (Cambridge, U.K.: Cambridge University Press, 1950).

20. R. H. Tawney, *Equality* (London: Allen & Unwin, 1931), p. 101.

Index